Say It Right in
FRENCH

Third Edition

guage Systems

uthor

New York   Chicago   San Francisco   Athens   London   Madrid
Mexico City   Milan   New Delhi   Singapore   Sydney   Toronto

1 2 3 4 5 6 7 8 9   LCR   23 22 21 20 19 18

ISBN   978-1-260-11632-8
MHID   1-260-11632-8

e-ISBN   978-1-260-11633-5
e-MHID   1-260-11633-6

Library of Congress Cataloging-in-Publication Data

Say it right in French / Easily Pronounced Language Systems — 2nd ed.
        p.   cm. — (Say it right)
    Includes index.
    Text in English and French.
    ISBN 978-0-07-176771-2 (alk. paper)
    1. French language—Pronunciation by foreign speakers.   2. French
language — Spoken French.   3. French language — Conversation and phrase
books — English.   I. Easily Pronounced Language Systems.   II. Clyde E.
Peters, Author.
PC2137.S39   2011
448.3'421—dc22   2011010675

Clyde Peters, author
Luc Nisset, illustrations
Betty Chapman, EPLS contributor, www.isayitright.com
Priscilla Leal Bailey, senior series editor
Michelle Lee, French consultant

Also available:
Say It Right in Chinese, Second Edition
Say It Right in Italian, Third Edition
Say It Right in Spanish, Third Edition

McGraw-Hill Education books are available at special quantity discounts to use
as premiums and sales promotions or for use in corporate training programs.
To contact a representative, please visit the Contact Us page at
www.mhprofessional.com.

McGraw-Hill Education Language Lab App

Streaming audio recordings (requiring Internet connection) of 500 words and
phrases from this book are available to help improve your pronunciation. Go to
www.mhlanguagelab.com to access the online version of this application, or
search the iTunes or Google Play app stores for the free mobile version of the app.

CONTENTS

INTRODUCTION

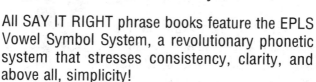

The SAY IT RIGHT FOREIGN
LANGUAGE PHRASE BOOK
SERIES has been developed
with the conviction that
learning to speak a foreign
language should be fun and easy!

All SAY IT RIGHT phrase books feature the EPLS
Vowel Symbol System, a revolutionary phonetic
system that stresses consistency, clarity, and
above all, simplicity!

Since this unique phonetic system is used in all
SAY IT RIGHT phrase books, you only have to
learn the VOWEL SYMBOL SYSTEM ONCE!

The SAY IT RIGHT series uses the easiest phrases
possible for English speakers to pronounce and
is designed to reflect how foreign languages are
used by native speakers.

You will be amazed at how confidence in your
pronunciation leads to an eagerness to talk to
other people in their own language.

Whether you want to learn a new language for
travel, education, business, study, or personal
enrichment, SAY IT RIGHT phrase books offer a
simple and effective method of pronunciation and
communication.

PRONUNCIATION GUIDE

Most English speakers are familiar with the French word **Merci**. This is how the correct pronunciation is represented in the EPLS Vowel Symbol System.

All French vowel sounds are assigned a specific non-changing symbol. When these symbols are used in conjunction with consonants and read normally, pronunciation of even the most difficult foreign word becomes incredibly EASY!.

On the following page are all the EPLS Vowel Symbols used in this book. They are EASY to LEARN since their sounds are familiar. Beneath each symbol are three English words which contain the sound of the symbol.

Practice pronouncing the words under each symbol until you mentally associate the correct vowel sound with the correct symbol. Most symbols are pronounced the way they look!

THE SAME BASIC SYMBOLS ARE USED IN ALL SAY IT RIGHT PHRASE BOOKS!

EPLS VOWEL SYMBOL SYSTEM

Ⓐ
Ace
Bake
Safe

ⒺⒺ
See
Feet
Meet

Ⓞ
Oak
Cold
Sold

ⓄⓄ
Cool
Pool
Too

ⓐ̆
Cat
Sad
Hat

ⓔ̆
Men
Red
Bed

ⓐⓗ
Calm
Hot
Off

ⓤⓗ
Fun
Sun
Run

ⓔⓦ
New
Few
Dew

This symbol represents the French letter **u**. Put your lips together as if to kiss and say **EE**.

Ⓞⓤ
Could
Would
Book

This symbol represents a unique sound found in the letters **eu** in French spelling. To master this sound you must listen to a native speaker's pronunciation. The **ou** sound in **could** is an effective substitute.

EPLS CONSONANTS

Consonants are letters like **T**, **D**, and **K**. They are easy to recognize and their pronunciation seldom changes. The following pronunciation guide letters represent some unique French consonant

Ɓ   Represents the French **r**. There is no English equivalent for this sound and it is very difficult to reproduce. It is pronounced far back in the throat and will take practice. It is essential to listen to a native speaker to master this sound. This Ɓ helps to remind you of the unique French r sound.

ZH Pronounce these EPLS letters like the **s** in mea**s**ure.

KW Pronounce these EPLS letters like the **qu** in **qu**it.

Nasalized Vowel Sounds

In French certain vowels are nasalized. This (ñ) immediately following a symbol tells you to nasalize the sound that the symbol represents. Try pinching your nose while pronouncing these words (try not to sound the **n** in the words):

Can	Zone	On	Sun
K@ñ	Z◎ñ	@hñ	S@hñ

PRONUNCIATION TIPS

- Each pronunciation guide word is broken into syllables. Read each word slowly, one syllable at a time, increasing speed as you become more familiar with the system.

- In general, equal emphasis is given to each syllable. Sometimes the French will slightly stress the last syllable in a sentence.

- Most of the symbols are pronounced the way they look!

- This phrase book provides a means to speak and be understood in French. **To perfect your French accent you must listen closely to French speakers and adjust your speech accordingly.**

- The pronunciation and word choices in this book were chosen for their simplicity and effectiveness.

- Some pronunciation guide letters are underlined (**Z I N**). This is simply to let you know that the underlined letter is a linking sound (called liaison) that connects two words.

- **SVP** is the abbreviation for **s'il vous plaît** which means "please" in French. You will see it used throughout the book.

ICONS USED IN THIS BOOK

KEY WORDS

You will find this icon at the beginning of chapters indicating key words relating to chapter content. These are important words to become familiar with.

PHRASEMAKER

The Phrasemaker icon provides the traveler with a choice of phrases that allows the user to make his or her own sentences.

Say It Right in FRENCH

ESSENTIAL WORDS AND PHRASES

Here are some basic words and phrases that will help you express your needs and feelings in **French**.

Hello

Bonjour

BOñ ZH∞R

How are you?

Comment allez-vous?

KO-MOñ Tã-LA-V∞

Fine / Very well

Très bien

TRA BEE-ahñ

And you?

Et vous?

A V∞

Good-bye

Au revoir

O Ruh-VWahR

Good morning

Bonjour

BOñ ZHOOR

Good evening

Bonsoir

BOñ SWahR

Good night

Bonne nuit

BuhN NWEE

Mr.

Monsieur

Muh-SYou

Mrs.

Madame

Mā-DāM

Miss

Mademoiselle

MāD-MWah-ZēL

Yes

Oui

WEE

No

Non

NOñ

Please

S'il vous plaît

SEEL VOO PLEE

Abbreviated SVP throughout the book

Thank you

Merci

MER-SEE

Excuse me

Pardon

PahR-DOñ

I'm sorry

Je suis désolé

ZHuh SWEE DA-ZO-LA

I'm a tourist.

Je suis touriste.

ZH**ⓤ** SW**Ⓔ** T**oo**-R**Ⓔ**ST

I do not speak French.

Je ne parle pas français.

ZH**ⓤ**N-**ⓤ** P**ⓐ**RL P**ⓐ** FR**ⓐ**ñ-S**Ⓐ**

I speak a little French.

Je parle un peu français.

ZH**ⓤ** P**ⓐ**RL **ⓤ**ñ P**ⓞⓤ** FR**ⓐ**ñ-S**Ⓐ**

Do you understand English?

Comprenez-vous l'anglais?

K**Ⓞ**ñ-PR**ⓤ**-N**Ⓐ**-V**oo** L**ⓐ**ñ-GL**Ⓐ**

I don't understand!

Je ne comprends pas!

ZH**ⓤ**N-**ⓤ** K**Ⓞ**ñ-PR**ⓐ**ñ P**ⓐ**

Please repeat.

Répétez s'il vous plaît.

R**Ⓔ**-P**Ⓔ**-T**Ⓐ** S**Ⓔ**L V**oo** PL**Ⓔ**

FEELINGS

I want…

Je veux…

ZH(uh) V(ou)…

I have…

J'ai…

ZH(A)…

I know.

Je sais.

ZH(uh) S(A)

I don't know.

Je ne sais pas.

ZH(uh)N S(A) P(ah)

I like it.

Je l'aime bien.

ZH(uh) L(e)M B(EE)-(ah)ñ

I don't like it.

Je ne l'aime pas bien.

ZH(uh)N-(uh) L(e)M P(ah) B(EE)-(a)ñ

I'm lost.

Je suis perdu.

ZH㋐ SW㋐ P㋐R-D㋐

I'm in a hurry.

Je suis pressé.

ZH㋐ SW㋐ PR㋐-S㋐

I'm tired.

Je suis fatigué.

ZH㋐ SW㋐ F㋐-T㋐-G㋐

I'm ill.

Je suis malade.

ZH㋐ SW㋐ M㋐-L㋐D

I'm hungry.

J'ai faim.

ZH㋐ F㋐ñ

I'm thirsty.

J'ai soif.

ZH㋐ SW㋐F

I'm angry.

Je suis en colère.

ZH㋐ SW㋐ Z㋐ñ K㋐-L㋐R

INTRODUCTIONS

My name is…

Je m'appelle…

ZHⓤⓗ Mⓐⓗ-Pⓔ̃L…

What's your name?

Comment vous appelez-vous?

KⓄ-MⓄñ Vⓞⓞ Zⓐⓗ-PLⒶ Vⓞⓞ

Where are you from?

D'où venez-vous?

Dⓞⓞ Vⓤⓗ-NⒶ Vⓞⓞ

Do you live here?

Habitez-vous ici?

ⓐⓗ-Bⓔⓔ-TⒶ Vⓞⓞ Zⓔⓔ-Sⓔⓔ

I just arrived.

Je viens d'arriver.

ZHⓤⓗ Vⓔⓔ-ⓐ̃ñ Dⓐⓗ-Bⓔⓔ-VⒶ

What hotel are you [staying] at?

Vous restez à quel hôtel?

Vⓞⓞ Bⓔ̃S-TⒶ ⓐⓗ Kⓔ̃ LⓄ-Tⓔ̃L

I'm at the…hotel.

Je reste à l'hôtel...

ZHⓤ Rẽ̄ST ⓐ LⓄ-Tẽ̄L...

It was nice to meet you.

Je suis enchanté de faire votre connaissance.

ZHⓤ SWẼ Zⓐñ-SHⓐñ-Tⓐ Dⓤ Fẽ̄R VⓄ-TRⓤ KⓄ-Nⓐ-Sⓐñ S

See you tomorrow.

A demain.

ⓐ Dⓤ-Mⓐ̃ñ

See you later.

A bientôt.

ⓐ BẼ-ⓐ̃ñ-TⓄ

Good luck!

Bonne chance!

Bⓤ N SHⓐñ S

In this book the symbol ⓤ is used to represent the French letter **"e"** in words such as **le, de,** etc. To master your French accent, have a French speaker pronounce these words and try to hone your accent accordingly.

THE BIG QUESTIONS

Who?

Qui?

K⒠

Who is it?

Qui est-ce?

K⒠ ⒠S

What?

Quoi?   Comment?

KW⒜   K⓪-M⓪ñ

What's that?

Qu'est-ce que c'est?

K⒠S-K⒰ S⒜

When?

Quand?

K⒜ñ

Where?

Où?

⓪⓪

Where is…?

Où est...?

Which?

Quel?   Quelle?   Quels?   Quelles?

KēL

Although spelled differently these are all pronounced the same.

Why?

Pourquoi?

PooB KWah

How?

Comment?

KO-MOñ

How much does it cost?

Combien?

KOñ-BEE-ahñ

How long?

Combien de temps?

KOñ-BEE-ahñ Duh Tahñ

ASKING FOR THINGS

The following phrases are valuable for directions, food, help, etc.

I would like…

Je voudrais...

ZH⒰ V⊚-DℝⒶ…

I need…

J'ai besoin...

ZHⒶ B⒰-ZWⓐñ…

Can you…?

Pouvez-vous...?

P⊚-VⒶ-V⊚…

When asking for things be sure to say <u>please</u> and <u>thank you</u>.

Please	**Thank you**
S'il vous plaît	Merci
SⒺL V⊚ PLⓔ	Mⓔℝ-SⒺ

PHRASEMAKER

Combine **I would like** with the
following phrases, and you will
have an effective way to ask for things.

I would like... please.

Je voudrais... s'il vous plaît.

ZH⓾ V⓪⓪-D⏣Ⓐ... SVP

▸ **more coffee**

  plus de café

  PLⓔⓦ D⓾ KⒶⓗ-FⒶ

▸ **some water**

  de l'eau

  D⓾ LⓄ

▸ **some ice**

  des glaçons

  DⒶ GLⓐ-SⓄñ

▸ **the menu**

  le menu

  L⓾ Mⓔ̆-Nⓔⓦ

PHRASEMAKER

Here are a few sentences you can
use when you feel the urge to say
I need or **Can you...**?

I need...

J'ai besoin... s'il vous plaît

ZH④ B⑩-ZW④ñ... SVP

▸ **help**

d'aide

D④D

▸ **directions**

de directions

D⑩ D㊞-B㊞K-S㊞-Oñ

▸ **more money**

de plus d'argent

D⑩ PL㊒ D㊀B-ZH㊀ñ

▸ **change**

de monnaie

D⑩ MO-N④

▸ **a lawyer**

d'un avocat

D⑩ñ N㊀-VO-K㊀

PHRASEMAKER

Can you...

Pouvez-vous... s'il vous plaît

Pⓞⓞ-VⒶ-Vⓞⓞ... SVP

▸ **help me?**

m'aider?

MⒶ-DⒶ

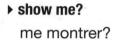

▸ **show me?**

me montrer?

Mⓤⓗ MⓄñ-TRⒶ

▸ **give me…?**

me donner...?

Mⓤⓗ DⓄ-NⒶ...

▸ **tell me…?**

me dire…?

Mⓤⓗ DⒺⒺR...

▸ **take me to…?**

m'emmener...?

MⓤⓗM-NⒶ...

ASKING THE WAY

No matter how independent
you are, sooner or later you'll
probably have to ask for
directions.

Where is...?

Où est...?

...

Is it near?

C'est près d'ici?

SⒶ PRⒶ DⒺ-SⒺ

Is it far?

C'est loin d'ici?

SⒶ LWⓐñ DⒺ-SⒺ

I'm lost!

Je suis perdu!

ZHⓊⓗ SWⒺ PⒺR-DⓊ

I'm looking for...

Je cherche...

ZHⓊⓗ SHⒺRSH...

PHRASEMAKER

Where is...

Où est...

⓪⓪ Ⓐ...

▶ **the telephone?**

le téléphone?

Lⓤⓗ TⒶ-LⒶ-FⓤⓗN

▶ **the beach?**

la plage?

LⒶⓗ PLⒶⓗZH

▶ **the hotel...?**

l'hôtel...?

LⓄ-TⒺL...

▶ **the train for...?**

le train pour...?

Lⓤⓗ TⒷⒶñ PⓄⓄⒷ...

Where are the restrooms?

Où sont les toilettes?

⓪⓪ SⓄñ LⒶ TWⒶⓗ-LⒺT

TIME

What time is it?

Quelle heure est-il?

Kⓔ LⓞⓤR Ⓐ-TⓔⓔL

Morning

Le matin

Lⓤⓗ Mⓐⓗ-Tⓐⓝ

Noon

Midi

Mⓔⓔ-Dⓔⓔ

Night

La nuit

Lⓐⓗ NWⓔⓔ

Today

Aujourd'hui

Ⓞ-ZHⓞⓞR-DWⓔⓔ

Tomorrow

Demain

Dⓤⓗ-Mⓐⓝ

This week

Cette semaine

SễT Sᵤₕ-MễN

This month

Ce mois

Sᵤₕ MWₐₕ

This year

Cette année

SễT ₐₕ-NⒶ

Now

Maintenant

MⒶñ-Tᵤₕ-Nₐₕñ

Soon

Bientôt

BⒺⒺ-ₐₕñ-TⓄ

Later

Plus tard

PLₑw TₐₕᴙB

Never

Jamais

ZHₐₕ-MⒶ

WHO IS IT?

I

Je

ZH⓾

You (formal)	**You** (informal)
Vous	Tu
V⓪⓪	T㋎
Use this form of **you** with people you don't know well.	Use this form of **you** with people you know well.

He

Il

㋍L

She

Elle

㋐L

We

Nous

N⓪⓪

They

Ils (m)	Elles (f)
㋍L	㋐L
A group of **men** only or a group of men and women.	A group of **women** only.

THE, A (AN), AND SOME

To use the correct form of **The**, **A** (**An**), or **Some**, you must know if the French word is masculine or feminine. Often you will have to guess! If you make a mistake, you will still be understood.

The

La

L(ah)

The before a singular feminine noun:
(La) woman is pretty.

Les

L(A)

The before a plural feminine noun:
(Les) women are pretty.

Le

L(uh)

The before a singular masculine noun:
(Le) boy is handsome.

Les

L(A)

The before a plural masculine noun:
(Les) boys are handsome.

A or An

Un

(uh)ñ

A or **an** before a singular masculine noun:
He is (un) man.

Une

(ew)N

A or **an** before a singular feminine noun:
She is (une) woman.

Some

Des

D(A)

Some before singular masculine nouns:
(Des) boys.

Des

D(A)

Some before singular feminine nouns:
(Des) women.

USEFUL OPPOSITES

Near	**Far**
Près de	Loin
PR⒜ D⒰	LW⒜ñ

Here	**There**
Ici	Là
⒠⒠-S⒠⒠	L⒜

Left	**Right**
A gauche	A droite
⒜ G⓪SH	⒜ DR̲W⒜T

A little	**A lot**
Un peu	Beaucoup
⒰ñ P⒪⒰	B⓪-K⒪⒪

More	**Less**
Plus	Moins
PL⒠⒲	MW⒜ñ

Big	**Small**
Grand (m) / Grande (f)	Petit (m) / Petite (f)
GR⒜ñ / GR⒜ND	P⒰-T⒠⒠ / P⒰-T⒠⒠T

Adjectives are masculine or feminine depending on the noun
they describe.

Open

Ouvert (m) / Ouverte (f)

oo-V❦R / oo-V❦RT

Closed

Fermé (m) / Fermée (f)

F❦R-M❹

Cheap

Bon marché

B❀ñ M❀B-SH❹

Expensive

Cher (m) / Chère (f)

SH❦R

Clean

Propre

PR❀-PR❿

Dirty

Sale

S❀L

Good

Bon (m) / Bonne (f)

B❀ñ / B❿N

Bad

Mauvais (m) / Mauvaise (f)

M❀-V❹ / M❀-V❦Z

Vacant

Libre

L❿❿-BR❿

Occupied

Occupé (m) / Occupée (f)

❀-K❿W-P❹´

Right

Avoir raison

❀-VW❀R
B❹-Z❀ñ

Wrong

Avoir tort

❀-VW❀R T❀R

WORDS OF ENDEARMENT

I love you.

Je t'aime.

ZH◍ TⒺM

My love

Mon amour

M◍ñ N@-M◍ℝ

My life

Ma vie

M@ VⒺ

My friend (to a male)

Mon ami (m)

M◍ñ N@-MⒺ

My friend (to a female)

Mon amie (f)

M◍ñ N@-MⒺ

Kiss me!

Embrasse-moi!

@ñ-BR@S MW@

WORDS OF ANGER

What do you want?

Qu'est-ce que vous voulez?

KĒS Kʰ Vᵒᵒ Vᵒᵒ-LⒶ

Leave me alone!

Laissez-moi tranquille!

LⒶ-SⒶ MWⁿᵃ TRⁿᵃⁿ-KĒL

Go away!

Allez-vous-en!

ᵃⁿ-LⒶ Vᵒᵒ-Zⁿᵃⁿ

Stop bothering me!

Ne me dérangez pas!

Nᵘʰ Mᵘʰ DⒶ-Rⁿᵃⁿ-ZHⒶ Pⁿᵃ

Be quiet!

Taisez-vous!

TⒶ-ZⒶ Vᵒᵒ

That's enough!

C'est assez!

SⒶ Tⁿᵃ-SⒶ

COMMON EXPRESSIONS

When you are at a loss for words but have the feeling you should say something, try one of these!

Who knows?

Qui sait?

K EE   S A

That's the truth!

C'est la vérité!

S A   L ah   V A-R EE-T A

Sure!	**Wow!**
Bien sûr!	Chouette!
B EE-añ S ew B	SH oo-é T

What's happening?

Qu'est-ce qui se passe?

K é S   K EE   S uh   P ah S

I think so.

Je pense que oui.

ZH uh   P ah ñ S   K uh   W EE

Cheers!

A votre santé!

ah VO-TRuh Sahñ-TA

Good luck!

Bonne chance!

BuhN SHahñS

With pleasure!

Avec plaisir!

ah-VēK PLA-ZEER

My goodness!

Mon dieu!

MOñ DYou

What a shame! / That's too bad!

C'est dommage!

SA DO-MahZH

Well done! Bravo!

Bravo!

BRah-VO

Never mind!

N'importe quoi!

Nāñ-PORT KWah

USEFUL COMMANDS

Stop!

Arrêtez!

ah-R℮-TA
___

Go!

Allez!

ah-LA
___

Wait!

Attendez!

ah-Tahñ-DA

___

Hurry!

Dépêchez-vous!

DA-P℮-SHA Voo
___

Slow down!

Lentement!

Lahñ T-Mahñ
___

Come here!

Venez ici!

Vuh-NA ZEE-SEE
___

Help!

Au secours!

O Suh-KooR
___

EMERGENCIES

Fire!

Au feu!

①-F⓪

Emergency!

L'urgence!

L⓮R-ZHⓐñS

Call the police!

Téléphonez à la police!

Tⓐ-Lⓐ-F⓪-Nⓐ ⓐ Lⓐ P⓪-LⓔⓔS

Call a doctor!

Téléphonez au médecin!

Tⓐ-Lⓐ-F⓪-Nⓐ ⓪ Mⓐ-D⓮-Sⓐñ

Call an ambulance!

Faites venir une ambulance!

F⓮T V⓮-NⓔⓔR ⓮N ⓐñ-B⓮-LⓐñS

I need help!

Au secours!

⓪ S⓮-K⓪⓪R

ARRIVAL

Passing through customs should be easy since there are usually agents available who speak English. You may be asked how long you intend to stay and if you have anything to declare.

- Have your passport ready.

- Be sure all documents are up-to-date.

- While in a foreign country, it is wise to keep receipts for everything you buy.

- Be aware that many countries will charge a departure tax when you leave. Your travel agent should be able to find out if this affects you.

- If you have connecting flights, be sure to reconfirm them in advance.

- Make sure your luggage is clearly marked inside and out.

- Take valuables and medicines in carry-on bags.

SIGNS TO LOOK FOR:

DOUANE (Customs)

FRONTIERE (Border)

LES BAGAGES (Baggage claim)

KEY WORDS

Baggage

Les bagages

L♳ B♳-G♳ZH

Customs

La douane

L♳ DW♳N

Documents

Les documents

L♳ D♳-K♳-M♳ñ

Passport

Le passeport

L♳ P♳S-P♳

Porter

Le porteur

L♳ P♳-T♳

Tax

La taxe

L♳ T♳KS

USEFUL PHRASES

Here is my passport.

Voici mon passeport.

VW@h-S⒠ M⍉ñ P⒜S-P⍉⒝

I have nothing to declare.

Je n'ai rien à déclarer.

ZH⒰ N⒜ ⒝⒠-@hñ @h

D⒜-KL@h-⒝⒜

I'm here on business.

Je suis en voyage d'affaires.

ZH⒰ SW⒠ Z@hñ

VW⍉ᵥ-Y@hZH D@h-F⒠⒝

I'm here on vacation.

Je suis en vacances.

ZH⒰ SW⒠ Z@hñ V⒜-K@hñS

Is there a problem?

Il y a un problème?

⒠L ⒠ @h ⒰hñ P⒝⍉-BL⒠M

PHRASEMAKER

I'll be staying…

Je vais rester…

ZH⓾ V④ R⓮S-T④…

▸ **one week**

une semaine

⓮N S⓾-M⓮N

▸ **two week**

deux semaines

D⓸ S⓾-M⓮N

▸ **one month**

un mois

⓾ñ MW④

▸ **two months**

deux mois

D⓸ MW④

USEFUL PHRASES

I need a porter!

J'ai besoin d'un porteur!

ZHⒶ BⓊⒽ-ZWⓐñ
DⓊñ PⓄB-TⓊB

Here is my luggage.

Voici mes bagages.

VWⓐ-SⒺⒺ MⒶ Bⓐ-GⓐZH

I'm missing a bag.

Je manque une valise.

ZHⓊⒽ MⓐñK ⒺWN Vⓐ-LⒺⒺS

Take my bags to the taxi, please.

Prenez mes valises au taxi, s'il vous plaît.

PBⓊⒽ-NⒶ MⒶ Vⓐ-LⒺⒺS Ⓞ
TⓐK-SⒺⒺ SVP

Thank you. This is for you.

Merci. C'est pour vous.

MⒺB-SⒺⒺ SⒶ PⓄⓄB VⓄⓄ

PHRASEMAKER

Where is...

Où est...

(oo) (A)...

▸ **customs?**

la douane?

L(ah) DW(ah)N

▸ **baggage claim?**

le depot de bagages?

L(uh) D(A)-P(O) D(uh) B(ã)-G(ah)ZH

▸ **the money exchange?**

le bureau d'échange?

L(uh) B(ew)-R(O) D(A)-SH(ah)ñZH

▸ **the taxi stand?**

la station de taxis?

L(ah) ST(ah)-S(EE)-(O)ñ D(uh) T(ã)K-S(EE)

▸ **the bus stop?**

l'arrêt d'autobus?

L(ah)-R(ẽ) D(O)-T(O)-B(ew)S

HOTEL
SURVIVAL

A wide selection of
accommodations, ranging
from the most basic to the
most extravagant, are
available wherever you travel
in France. When booking your
room, find out what amenities
are included for the price you
pay.

- Make reservations well in advance and get
  written confirmation of your reservations
  before you leave home.

- Always have identification ready when
  checking in.

- Do not leave valuables, prescriptions, or cash
  in your room when you are not there.

- Electrical items like blow-dryers may need an
  adapter. Your hotel may be able to provide
  one, but to be safe, take one with you.

- **Service Compris** or **Toutes Taxes Comprises**
  on your bill means the tip is already included,
  except for the bellman.

KEY WORDS

Hotel Baggage

L'hôtel

LO-TëL

Bellman

Un garçon d'hôtel

uhñ GahR-SOñ DO-TëL

Maid

Une domestique

ewN DO-MëS-TEEK

Message

Le message

Luh Më-SahZH

Reservation

La réservation

Lah Rë-SëR-Vah-SEE-Oñ

Room service

Le service dans les chambres

Luh SëR-VEES Dahñ LA SHahñ-BRuh

CHECKING IN

My name is…

Je m'appelle...

ZH⓪ M⓪-P⓮L

I have a reservation.

J'ai réservé.

ZH④ R⓮-S⓮R-V④

Have you any vacancies?

Vous avez des chambres libres?

V⓪ Z⓪-V④ D④
SH⓪ñ-BR⓾ L⓮-BR⓾

What is the charge?

Quel est le prix?

K⓮ L④ L⓾ PR⓮

Is there room service?

Il y a le service dans les chambres?

⓮L ⓮ ⓪ L⓾ S⓮R-V⓮S
D⓪ñ L④ SH⓪ñ-BR⓾

My room key, please.

Ma clé de chambre, s'il vous plaît.

M⓪ KL⓮ D⓾ SH⓪ñ-BR⓾ SVP

PHRASEMAKER

I would like a room...

Je voudrais une chambre...

ZH@ V@-DR@ @N SH@ñ-BR@...

▶ **with a bath**

avec une salle de bains

@-V@K @N S@L D@ B@ñ

▶ **with one bed**

à un lit

@ @ñ L@

▶ **with two beds**

à deux lits

@ D@ L@

▶ **with a shower**

avec une douche

@-V@K @N D@SH

▶ **with a view**

avec la vue

@-V@K L@ V@

USEFUL PHRASES

Where is the dining room?
Où est la salle à manger?

⓪⓪ Ⓐ Lⓐⓗ SⓐⓗL ⓐⓗ Mⓐⓗñ-ZHⒶ

Are meals included?
Est-ce que les repas sont compris?

ⓔS-Kⓤⓗ LⒶ Rⓤⓗ-Pⓐⓗ
SⓄñ KⓄñ-PRⓔⓔ

What time is breakfast?
A quelle heure est le petit déjeuner?

ⓐⓗ Kⓔ LⓄⓤR Ⓐ Lⓤⓗ Pⓤⓗ-Tⓔⓔ
DⒶ-ZHⓄⓤ-NⒶ

What time is lunch?
A quelle heure est le déjeuner?

ⓐⓗ Kⓔ LⓄⓤR Ⓐ
Lⓤⓗ DⒶ-ZHⓄⓤ-NⒶ

What time is dinner?
A quelle heure est le dîner?

ⓐⓗ Kⓔ LⓄⓤR Ⓐ Lⓤⓗ Dⓔⓔ-NⒶ

Are there any messages for me?

Y a-t-il des messages pour moi?

ⒺⒺ ⓐⓗ TⒺⒺL DⒶ Mⓔ̃-SⓐⓗZH
PⓄⓄR MWⓐⓗ

Please wake me at…

Veuillez me réveiller à…

VⓄⓤ-YⒶ Mⓤⓗ Rⓔ̃-Vⓔ̃-YⒶ ⓐⓗ…

6:00
six heures
SⒺⒺ Z̲ⓄⓤR

6:30
six heures et demie
SⒺⒺ Z̲ⓄⓤR Ⓐ Dⓤⓗ-MⒺⒺ

7:00
sept heures
Sⓔ̃ T̲ⓄⓤR

7:30
sept heures et demie
Sⓔ̃ T̲ⓄⓤR Ⓐ Dⓤⓗ-MⒺⒺ

8:00
huit heures
WⒺⒺ T̲ⓄⓤR

8:30
huit heures et demie
WⒺⒺ T̲ⓄⓤR Ⓐ Dⓤⓗ-MⒺⒺ

9:00
neuf heures
NⓄⓤ VⓄⓤR

9:30
neuf heures et demie
NⓄⓤ VⓄⓤR Ⓐ Dⓤⓗ-MⒺⒺ

PHRASEMAKER

I need…

J'ai besoin...

ZHⒶ B(uh)-ZW(ah)ñ...

▸ **a babysitter**

d'une garde-bébé

D(ew)N G(ah)R̰D BⒶ-BⒶ

▸ **a bellman**

d'un garçon d'hôtel

D(uh)ñ G(ah)R̰-SⓄñ DⓄ-T(ĕ)L

▸ **more blankets**

de plus de couvertures

D(uh) PL(ew) D(uh) K(oo)-V(ĕ)R̰-T(ew)R̰

▸ **a hotel safe**

d'un coffre-fort

D(uh)ñ KⓄ-FR̰(uh) FⓄR̰

▸ **ice cubes**

de glaçons

D(uh) GL(ă)-SⓄñ

▸ **an extra key**

d'un clé supplémentaire

Duhñ KLA Sew-PLA-Muhñ-TёR

▸ **a maid**

de domestique

Duh DO-MёS-TEEK

▸ **the manager**

de directeur (m)   de directrice (f)

Duh DEE-RёK-TouR   Duh DEE-RёK-TREES

▸ **clean sheets**

de draps propre

Duh DRah PRO-PRuh

▸ **soap**

de savon

Duh Sah-VOñ

▸ **toilet paper**

de papier hygiénique

Duh Pah-PEE-A EE-ZHEE-A-NEEK

▸ **more towels**

de plus de serviettes

Duh PLew Duh SёR-VEE-ёT

PHRASEMAKER
(PROBLEMS)

There is no…

Il n'y a pas...

ⒺL NYⓐ Pⓐ...

▸ **electricity**

d'électricité

DⒶ-LⓔK-TⓇⒺⒺ-SⒺⒺ-TⒶ

▸ **heat**

de chauffage

Dⓤ SHⓄ-Fⓐ ZH

▸ **hot water**

d'eau chaude

DⓄ SHⓄD

▸ **light**

de lumière

Dⓤ LⓄⓄM-YⓔⓇ

▸ **toilet paper**

de papier hygiénique

Dⓤ Pⓐ-PⒺⒺ-Ⓐ ⒺⒺ-ZHⒺⒺ-Ⓐ-NⒺⒺK

PHRASEMAKER
(SPECIAL NEEDS)

Do you have…

Avez-vous…

ⓐ-ⓋⒶ Ⓥ⊚…

▸ **an elevator?**

un ascenseur?

ⓤñ N̲ⓐ-Sⓐñ-SⓞⓊⱤ

▸ **a ramp?**

une rampe?

ⓔⓦN Ɽⓐ︎MP

▸ **a wheelchair?**

un fauteuil roulant?

ⓤñ FⓄ-TⓞⓊ-Yⓤ Ɽ⊚-Lⓐñ

▸ **facilities for the disabled?**

des aménagements pour les
handicapés?

DⒶ Z̲ⓐ-MⒶ-Nⓐ︎ZH-Mⓐñ P⊚Ɽ

LⒶ ⓐN-DⒺⒺ-Kⓐ-PⒶ

CHECKING OUT

The bill, please.

Voulez-vous me préparer la note, s'il vous plaît.

V⓪-L④-V⓪ Mⓤ PR④-Pⓐ-R④

Lⓐ N⓪T svp

Is this bill correct?

Il y a une erreur dans la note?

ⒺL Ⓔ ⓐ ⓔⓦN ⓔR-⓪R

Dⓐñ Lⓐ N⓪T

Do you accept credit cards?

Acceptez-vous les cartes de crédit?

ⓐ-SⓔP-T④ V⓪ L④ KⓐRT

Dⓤ KR④-DⒺ

Could you have my luggage brought down?

Pouvez-vous faire descendre mes bagages?

P⓪-V④-V⓪ FⓔR D④-Sⓐñ-DRⓤ

M④ B⓪-GⓐZH

Can you call a taxi for me?

Appelez-moi un taxi, s'il vous plaît.

@h-PL@ MW@h @hñ T@K-S@ svp

I had a very good time!

Je me suis bien amusé!

ZH@ M@ SW@ B@-@hñ
N@-M@w-Z@

Thanks for everything.

Merci pour tout.

M@B-S@ P@B T@

I'll see you next time.

A la prochaine.

@h L@ PR@-SH@N

Good-bye.

Au revoir.

@ R@-VW@B

RESTAURANT SURVIVAL

From sidewalk cafés to the most elegant restaurants, you will find a delectable assortment of French cuisine. Bon appetit!

- Breakfast, **le petit déjeuner**, is usually small and served at your hotel. Lunch, **le déjeuner**, is normally served from 12:30 PM to 3 PM. Dinner, **le dîner**, begins after 7 PM and can extend for hours. It is more formal than lunch and a time for enjoyment of great French cuisine and wine!

- You will find menus posted outside eating establishments and they may contain the following statements: **Service Compris** (service included) or **Non Compris** (service not included). Most restaurants include tax and a service charge.

- Some restaurants may charge for meals by **prix-fixe,** a set menu usually including two or three courses for one set price or **a la carte**.

- Café prices will be more expensive in high tourist areas. Prices can vary by counter or table seating.

KEY WORDS

Breakfast

le petit déjeuner

L⑩ P⑩-T㏄ D④-ZH⑩-N④

Lunch

le déjeuner

L⑩ D④-ZH⑩-N④

Dinner

le dîner

L⑩ D㏄-N④

Waiter

Monsieur

M⑩-SY⑩

Waitress

Mademoiselle

M⑩D-MW⑩-Z㏄L

Restaurant

le restaurant

L⑩ B㏄S-T⑩-B⑩ñ

USEFUL PHRASES

A table for...

Une table à...

ⓔwN TⓐB-Lⓤh ⓐh...

2	4	6
deux	quatre	six
Dⓞⓤ	Kⓐ-Tⓡ ⓤh	SⓔⓔS

The menu, please.

La carte, s'il vous plaît.

Lⓐh KⓐhⓡT SVP

Separate checks, please.

L'addition individuelle, s'il vous plaît.

Lⓐh-Dⓔⓔ-Sⓔⓔ-Oñ

ⓐhñ-Dⓔⓔ-Vⓔⓔ-Jⓞⓞ-ⓔL SVP

We are in a hurry.

Nous sommes pressés.

Nⓞⓞ SⓤhM Pⓡ ⓔ-Sⓐ

What do you recommend?

Qu'est-ce que vous recommandez?

Kⓔ S Kⓤh Vⓞⓞ ⓡⓤh-KO-Mⓐhñ-Dⓐ

Please bring me...

Apportez-moi... s'il vous plaît.

@-P⊙℞-T④ MW@... SVP

Please bring us...

Apportez-nous... s'il vous plaît.

@-P⊙℞-T④ N⊙⊙... SVP

I'm hungry.

J'ai faim.

ZH④ F@ñ

I'm thirsty.

J'ai soif.

ZH④ SW@F

Is service included?

Le service est compris?

L⊎ S℮℞-V℮℮S ④ K⊙ñ-P℞℮℮

The bill, please.

L'addition, s'il vous plaît.

L@-D℮℮-S℮℮-⊙ñ SVP

PHRASEMAKER

Ordering beverages is easy and a
great way to practice your French! In many foreign
countries you may have to request ice with drinks.

Please bring me...

Apportez-moi... s'il vous plaît.

@h-P@B-T@ MW@h... SVP

▶ **coffee**   ▶ **tea**

du café   du thé

D@w K@h-F@   D@w T@

▶ **with cream**

avec de la crème

@h-V@K D@h L@h KB@M

▶ **with sugar**

avec du sucre

@h-V@K D@w S@w-KB@h

▶ **with lemon**

avec du citron

@h-V@K D@w S@-TB@ñ

▶ **with ice**

avec de la glace

@h-V@K D@h L@h GL@S

Soft drinks

Les sodas

LⒶ SⓄ-Dⓐⓗ

Milk

Le lait

Lⓤⓗ LⒶ

Hot chocolate

Le chocolat chaud

Lⓤⓗ SHⓄ-KⓄ-Lⓐⓗ SHⓄ

Juice

Le jus

Lⓤⓗ ZHⓔⓦ

Orange juice

Le jus d'orange

Lⓤⓗ ZHⓔⓦ DⓄ-RⓐⓗñZH

Ice water

L'eau glacée

LⓄ GLⓐ̃-SⒶ

Mineral water

L'eau minérale

LⓄ MⒺⒺ-NⒶ-RⓐⓗL

AT THE BAR

Bartender

Le bar man

L⬤ B⬤R M⬤N

The wine list

La carte des vins

L⬤ K⬤RT D⬤ V⬤ñ

Cocktail

Le cocktail

L⬤ K⬤K-T⬤L

On the rocks

Aux glaçons

⬤ GL⬤-S⬤ñ

Straight

Sans glaçons

S⬤ñ GL⬤-S⬤ñ

With lemon

Avec du citron

⬤-V⬤K D⬤ S⬤-TR⬤ñ

PHRASEMAKER

I would like a glass of...

Je voudrais un verre...

ZHⓤⓗ Vⓞⓞ-DRⒶ ⓤⓗñ VⒺⓇ...

▸ **champagne**

de champagne

Dⓤⓗ SHⓐⓗñ-Pⓐⓗñ-Yⓤⓗ

▸ **beer**

de bière

Dⓤⓗ BⒺⒺ-ⒺⓇ

▸ **wine**

de vin

Dⓤⓗ VⒶñ

▸ **red wine**

de vin rouge

Dⓤⓗ VⒶñ RⓞⓞZH

▸ **white wine**

de vin blanc

Dⓤⓗ VⒶñ BLⓐⓗñ

ORDERING
BREAKFAST

In France **"le petit déjeuner"** (breakfast) is usually small, consisting of a croissant or French bread with butter and jam and accompanied by café au lait, hot tea, or hot chocolate.

Bread

Le pain

L⓾ P⒜ñ

Toast

Le toast

L⓾ T◎ST

---

with butter

avec du beurre

⒜-V⒠K D⒠w B◎◎R

---

with jam

avec de la confiture

⒜-V⒠K D⓾ L⒜ K◎ñ-F⒠E-T⒠wR

Cereal

Les céréales

L⒜ S⒜-R⒜-⒜L

PHRASEMAKER

I would like…

Je voudrais...

ZH⒰ V⓪⓪-DℝⒶ…

▸ **two eggs…**

deux oeufs...

D⓪⓪ Z⓪⓪…

▸ **scrambled**

brouillés

BℝⓄⓄ-YⒶ

▸ **fried**

sur le plat

S⒠ℝ L⒰ PLⓐ

▸ **with bacon**

avec du bacon

ⓐ-VⒺK D⒠ BⒶ-K⒰N

▸ **with ham**

avec du jambon

ⓐ-VⒺK D⒠ ZHⓐM-BⓄñ

▸ **with potatoes**

avec des pommes de terre

ⓐ-VⒺK DⒶ P⒰M D⒰ TⒺℝ

LUNCH AND DINNER

Although you are encouraged to
sample great French cuisine, it is
important to be able to order foods
you are familiar with. This section
will provide words and phrases to
help you.

I would like...

Je voudrais...

ZH⒰ V⓪-DⓇⒶ...

We would like...

Nous voudrions...

N⓪ V⓪-DⓇⒺ-Oñ...

Bring us... please.

Apportez-nous... s'il vous plaît.

⒜-P⓪B-TⒶ N⓪... SVP

The lady would like...

La madame voudrait...

L⒜ M⒜-D⒜M V⓪-DⓇⒶ...

The gentleman would like...

Le monsieur voudrait...

L⒰ M⒰-SY⒪ V⓪-DⓇⒶ...

STARTERS

Appetizers

Les hors d'oeuvres

L(A) Z(O)R-D(ou)-VR(uh)

Bread and butter

Le pain et le beurre

L(uh) P(a)ñ (A) L(uh) B(ou)R

Cheese

Le fromage

L(uh) FR(O)-M(ah)ZH

Fruit

Le fruit

L(uh) FRW(EE)

Salad

La salade

L(ah) S(A)-L(ah)D

Soup

La soupe

L(ah) S(oo)P

MEATS

Bacon
Le bacon
L⬤ B⬤-K⬤N

Beef
Le boeuf
L⬤ B⬤F

Beef steak
Le bifteck
L⬤ B⬤F-T⬤K

Ham
Le jambon
L⬤ ZH⬤M-B⬤ñ

Lamb
L'agneau
L⬤-NY⬤

Pork
Le porc
L⬤ P⬤R

Veal
Le veau
L⬤ V⬤

POULTRY

Baked chicken

Le poulet au four

L(uh) P(oo)-L(A) (O) F(oo)R

Broiled chicken

Le poulet grillé

L(uh) P(oo)-L(A) GR(EE)-Y(A)

Fried chicken

Le poulet frit

L(uh) P(oo)-L(A) FR(EE)

Duck

Le canard

L(uh) K(a)-N(ah)R

Goose

L'oie

LW(oo)-(ah)

Turkey

La dinde

L(ah) D(ah)ñD

SEAFOOD

Fish

Le poisson

L⓾ PW⓮-S⓪ñ

Lobster

Le homard

L⓾ ⓪-Mⓐ⓱

Oysters

Les huîtres

Lⓐ Z̲W⓮-TR⓾

Salmon

Le saumon

L⓾ S⓾-M⓪ñ

Shrimp

Les crevette

Lⓐ KR⓾-V⓮T

Trout

La truite

Lⓐ TRW⓮T

Tuna

Le thon

L⓾ T⓪ñ

OTHER ENTREES

Sandwich
Le sandwich

L⒰ S⒜ñ-W⒠⒠SH

Hot dog
Le hot-dog

L⒰ H⒜T D⒜G

Hamburger
Le hamburger

L⒰ ⒜M-B⒠R-G⒠R

French fries
Les frites

L⒜ FR⒠⒠T

Pasta
Les pâtes

L⒜ P⒜T

Pizza
La pizza

L⒜ P⒠⒠-Z⒜

VEGETABLES

Carrots

Les carottes

L Ⓐ Kⓐⓗ-ⓇⓄT

Corn

Le maïs

L ⓤⓗ Mⓐⓗ-ⒺⒺS

Mushrooms

Les champignons

L Ⓐ SHⓐⓗñ-PⒺⒺ-NYⓄñ

Onions

Les oignons

L Ⓐ ZⓄ-NYⓄñ

Potato

La pomme de terre

L ⓐⓗ PⓤⓗM Dⓤⓗ TⓔⓇ

Rice

Le riz

L ⓤⓗ ⓇⒺⒺ

Tomato

La tomate

L ⓐⓗ TⓄ-MⓐⓗT

FRUITS

Apple

La pomme

L@h P@hM

Banana

La banane

L@h B@h-N@hN

Grapes

Les raisins

L@ R@-Z@ñ

Lemon

Le citron

L@h S@-TR@ñ

Orange

L'orange

L@-R@hñZH

Strawberry

La fraise

L@h FR@Z

Watermelon

La pastèque

L@h P@hS-T@K

DESSERT

Desserts

Les desserts

L⒜ D⒜-S⒤⒝

Apple pie

La tarte aux pommes

L⒜ T⒜RT ⓞ P⒰M

Cherry pie

La tarte aux cerises

L⒜ T⒜RT ⓞ S⒤-R⒠S

Pastries

Les pâtisseries

L⒜ P⒜-T⒠⒠-S⒤-R⒠⒠

Candy

Les bonbons

L⒜ Bⓞñ Bⓞñ

Ice cream

La glace

L(ah) GL(ä)S

Ice-cream cone

Le cône

L(uh) K(O)N

Chocolate

Au chocolat

(O) SH(O)-K(O)-L(ah)

Strawberry

A la fraise

(ah) L(ah) FR(ĕ)Z

Vanilla

A la vanille

(ah) L(ah) V(ah)-N(EE)

CONDIMENTS

Butter
Le beurre
L⓾ B⓾R

Ketchup
Le ketchup
L⓾ K⓾T-CH⓾P

Mayonnaise
La mayonnaise
L⓾ M⓾-Y⓾-N⓾Z

Mustard
La moutarde
L⓾ M⓾-T⓾RD

Salt	**Pepper**
Le sel	Le poivre
L⓾ S⓾L	L⓾ PW⓾-VR⓾

Sugar
Le sucre
L⓾ S⓾-KR⓾

Vinegar and oil
La vinaigrette
L⓾ V⓾-N⓾-GR⓾T

SETTINGS

A cup
Une tasse
N TS

A glass
Un verre
ñ VR

A spoon
Une cuillère
N KW-R

A fork
Une fourchette
N FR-SHT

A knife
Un couteau
ñ K-T

A plate
Une assiette
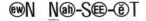N N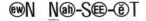-S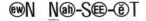-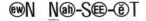T

A napkin
Une serviette
N SR-V-T

HOW DO YOU WANT IT COOKED?

Baked

Cuit au four

KW_{EE}T Ⓞ F_{OO}R

Broiled

Grillé

GR_{EE}-Y_A

Steamed

A l'étuvée

_{ah} L_A-T_{ew}-V_A

Fried

Frit

FR_{EE}

Rare

Saignant

S_A-NY_{ah}ñ

Medium

A point

_{ah} PW_{ah}ñ

Well done

Bien cuit

B_{EE}-_{ah}ñ KW_{EE}

PROBLEMS

I didn't order this.

Je n'ai pas commandé ceci.

ZH⒰ N⒜ P⒜
K⒪-M⒜N-D⒜ S⒰-S⒠

Is the bill correct?

Il y a une erreur dans la note?

⒠L ⒠ ⒜ ⒠N ⒠B-R⒪B
D⒜ñ L⒜ N⒪T

Please bring me.

Apportez-moi... s'il vous plaît.

⒜-P⒪B-T⒜ MW⒜... SVP

GETTING AROUND

Getting around in a foreign country can be an adventure in itself! Taxi and bus drivers do not always speak English, so it is essential to be able to give simple directions. The words and phrases in this chapter will help you get where you're going.

- The best way to get a taxi is to ask your hotel or restaurant to call one for you or go to the nearest taxi stand, **Stationnement de Taxi.** Tipping is customary.

- Trains are used frequently by visitors to Europe. They are efficient and provide connections between large cities and towns throughout the country. Arrive early to allow time for ticket purchasing and checking in, and remember, trains leave on time!

- **Le Métro** or subway is an inexpensive underground train system in Paris. It is easily accessible and a great way to get around. **"M"** signifies a metro stop!

- Check with your travel agent about special rail passes that allow unlimited travel within a set period of time.

KEY WORDS

Airport

L' aéroport

L ah -A-RO-POR

Bus Station / Bus Stop

Le gare routière
L'arrêt de bus

L uh G ah R R oo -T EE - ê R

L ah -R ê   D uh   B ew S

Car Rental Agency

L'agence de location

L ah -ZH ah ñ S D uh   LO-K ah -S EE -O ñ

Subway Station

Le métro

L uh   M A -TR O

Taxi Stand

La station de taxis

L ah   ST ah -S EE -O ñ   D uh   T ä K-S EE

Train Station

La gare

L ah   G ah R

AIR TRAVEL

Arrivals
Les arrivées
L Ⓐ   Z-ah-REE-VⒶ

Departures
Les départs
L Ⓐ   DⒶ-Pah-R

Flight number
Le vol numéro
L uh   VOL   N-ew-MⒶ-RO

Airline
La ligne aérienne
L ah   L-EE-N-Y-uh   ah-Ⓐ-R-EE-ⓔN

The gate
La porte
L ah   PORT

Information
Les renseignements
L Ⓐ   R-ah-ñ-S-ⓔN-Y-uh-M-ah-ñ

Ticket (airline)
Le billet
L uh   B-EE-YⒶ

Reservations
Les réservations
L Ⓐ   RⒶ-S-ⓔR-V-ah-S-EE-Oñ

PHRASEMAKER

I would like a seat…
Je voudrais une place...
ZH⓾ V⊕⊕-D℞Ⓐ ⓮N PLⓐS...

▶ **in first class**
à première classe
Ⓐ P℞⓾M-YⒺ℞ KLⓐS

▶ **in the no-smoking section**
dans la zone non fumeurs
Dⓐñ Lⓐ Z⊕N N⊕ñ F⓮-M⊕⊕℞

▶ **next to the window**
à côté de la fenêtre
Ⓐ K⊕-TⒶ D⓾ Lⓐ
F⓾-NⒺ-T℞⓾

▶ **on the aisle**
au couloir
⊕ K⊕⊕L-Wⓐ℞

▶ **near the exit**
près de la sortie
P℞Ⓐ D⓾ Lⓐ S⊕℞-TⒺⒺ

BY BUS

Bus

L'autobus

L⓪-T⓪-B⒠S

Where is the bus stop?

Où est l'arrêt d'autobus?

⓪⓪   Ⓐ   Lⓐ-Rⓔ̆   D⓪-T⓪-B⒠S

Do you go to…?

Vous allez à...?

V⓪⓪   Zⓐ-LⒶ   ⓐ...

What is the fare?

C'est combien?

SⒶ   KⓄñ-Bⓔⓔ-ⓐñ

Do I need exact change?

Est-ce que j'ai besoin de monnaie précise?

ⓔ̆S-Kⓤ   ZHⒶ   Bⓤ-ZWⓐñ   Dⓤ

M⓪-NⒶ   PℝⒶ-SⓔⓔS

How often do the buses run?

Les autobus sont tous les combien?

LⒶ   Z⓪-T⓪-B⒠S   SⓄñ   T⓪⓪   LⒶ

KⓄñ-Bⓔⓔ-ⓐñ

PHRASEMAKER

Please tell me...

S'il vous plaît dites-moi...

SⒺL VⓄⓄ PLⓔ DⒺT MWⓐⓗ...

▸ **which bus goes to...**

quel autobus va à...

Kⓔ LⓄ-TⓄ-BⓔⓦS Vⓐⓗ ⓐⓗ...

▸ **what time the bus leaves**

à quelle heure est-ce que l'autobus départ

ⓐⓗ Kⓔ LⓄⓊⓇ ⓔS-KⓊⓗ LⓄ-TⓄ-BⓔⓦS DⒶ-PⓐⓗⓇ

▸ **where the bus stop is**

où est l'arrêt d'autobus

ⓄⓄ Ⓐ Lⓐⓗ-Ⓡⓔ DⓄ-TⓄ-BⓔⓦS

▸ **where to get off**

où est-ce qu'il faut descendre

ⓄⓄ ⓔS-KⒺL FⓄ DⒶ-Sⓐⓗñ-DⓇⓊⓗ

BY CAR

Fill it up.

Faites le plein.

F̃ẽT L⑩ PL⒜ñ

Can you help me?

Vous pouvez m'aider?

V⑩ P⑩-V⒜ M⒜-D⒜

My car won't start.

Ma voiture ne démarre pas.

M⒜ VW⒜-T⑩R N⑩ D⒜-M⒜B P⒜

Can you fix it?

Vous pouvez la réparer?

V⑩ P⑩-V⒜ L⒜ B⒜-P⒜-B⒜

What will it cost?

Combien est-ce que cela coûte?

K⑩ñ-B̃EE-⒜ñ ẽS-K⑩ S⑩-L⒜ K⑩T

How long will it take?

Ça va prendre combien de temps?

S⒜ V⒜ PB⒜ñ-DB⑩
K⑩ñ-B̃EE-⒜ñ D⑩ T⒜ñ

PHRASEMAKER

Please check…

S'il vous plaît vérifiez...

S℮℮L V℗℗ PL℮̈ V℗-Ṟ℮℮-FY℗....

▸ **the battery**

la batterie

L℗ B℗-T℮̈-Ṟ℮℮

▸ **the brakes**

les freins

L℗ FṞ℗N

▸ **the oil**

l'huile

L℮ẇ-℮℮L

▸ **the tires**

les pneus

L℗ P℺-N℗℗

▸ **the water**

l'eau

L℗

SUBWAYS AND TRAINS

Where is the subway station?

Où est le métro?

ⓞⓞ Ⓐ Lⓤⓗ MⒶ-TⓇⓄ

Where is the train station?

Où est la gare?

ⓞⓞ Ⓐ Lⓐⓗ GⓐⓗR

A one-way ticket, please.

Un aller, s'il vous plaît.

ⓤⓗñ Nⓐⓗ-LⒶ svp

A round trip ticket.

Un aller et retour.

ⓤⓗñ Nⓐⓗ-LⒶ Ⓐ Rⓤⓗ-TⓞⓞR

First class

Première classe

PRⓤⓗM-YⒺⓇ KLⓐS

Second class

Deuxième classe

Dⓞⓤ-ZⒺⒺ-ⒺM KLⓐS

Which train do I take to go to…?

Quel train est-ce que je prends
pour aller à...?

KēL TRãÑ ēS-Kuh ZHuh PRãÑ
POOR ah-LA ah...

What is the fare?

C'est combien?

SA KOÑ-BEE-ahÑ

Is this seat taken?

La place est libre?

Lah PLahS A LEE-BRuh

Do I have to change trains?

Est-ce qu'il faut changer de train?

ēS-KēL FO SHahÑ-ZHA Duh TRãÑ

Does this train stop at…?

Est-ce que ce train s'arrête à...?

ēS-Kuh Suh TRãÑ Sah-Bē Tah...

Where are we?

Où sommes-nous?

OO SOM NOO

BY TAXI

Can you call a taxi for me?

Appelez-moi un taxi, s'il vous plaît.

ⓐⓗ-PLⒶ MWⓐⓗ ⓤⓗñ TⓐⓗK-SⒺⒺ SVP

Are you available?

Vous êtes libre?

VⓄⓄ ZⓔⓣT LⒺⒺ-BRⓤⓗ

I want to go…

Je voudrais aller...

ZHⓤⓗ VⓄⓄ-DRⒶ ⓐⓗ-LⒶ...

Stop here, please.

Arrêtez ici, s'il vous plaît.

ⓐⓗ-Rⓔⓣ-TⒶ ZⒺⒺ-SⒺⒺ SVP

Please wait.

Attendez, s'il vous plaît.

ⓐⓗ-Tⓐⓗñ-DⒶ SVP

How much do I owe you?

Combien est-ce que je dois?

KⓄñ-BⒺⒺ-ⓐⓗñ ⓔⓣS-Kⓤⓗ ZHⓤⓗ DWⓐⓗ

PHRASEMAKER

I would like to go…

Je voudrais aller...

ZH⒰ V⒨-DR⒜ Z⒜-L⒜...

▸ **to this address**

à cet adresse

⒜ S⒠T ⒜-DR⒠S

▸ **to the airport**

à l'aéroport

⒜ L⒜-⒜-R⒪-P⒪R

▸ **to the bank**

à la banque

⒜ L⒜ B⒜NK

▸ **to the hotel**

à l'hôtel

⒜ L⒪-T⒠L

▸ **to the hospital**

à l'hôpital

⒜ L⒪-P⒠-T⒜L

▸ **to the subway station**

au métro

⒪ M⒜-TR⒪

SHOPPING

Whether you plan a major shopping spree or just need to purchase some basic necessities, the following information is useful.

- Palais de Congrès de Paris and Forum des Halles are popular shopping centers in Paris.

- Department stores are open Monday through Saturday between 9:30 AM and 6:00 PM. Smaller stores may close for lunch between noon and 2:00 PM. Outdoor markets are only open for limited hours.

- There are three main flea markets in Paris providing wonderful opportunities to find treasures.

- Always keep receipts for everything you buy!

SIGNS TO LOOK FOR:

BOULANGERIE (Bakery)

BUREAU DE TABAC (Smoke shop, stamps)

CARTES POSTALES (Post cards)

GRAND MAGASIN (Department store)

CHAUSSURES (Shoes)

SUPERMARCHE (Supermarket)

KEY WORDS

Credit card

La carte de crédit

L@h K@hRT D@h KR@-D@E

Money

L'argent

L@hR-ZH@hñ

Receipt

Le reçu

L@h R@h-S@w

Sale

La vente

L@h V@hñT

Store

Le magasin

L@h M@-G@-Z@hñ

Travelers' checks

Les chèques de voyage

L@ SH@K D@h VW@-Y@hZH

USEFUL PHRASES

Do you sell…?

Est-ce que vous vendez…?

ⒺS-Kⓤ Vⓞⓞ Vⓐⓝ-DⒶ…

Do you have…?

Avez-vous…?

ⓐ-VⒶ Vⓞⓞ…

I want to buy…

Je voudrais acheter…

ZHⓤ Vⓞⓞ-DRⒶ ⓐSH-TⒶ…

How much?

Combien?

KⓄⓝ-BⒺⒺ-ⓐⓝ

When are the shops open?

Quand est-ce que les boutiques s'ouvrent?

Kⓐⓝ TⒺS-Kⓤ LⒶ
Bⓞⓞ-TⒺⒺK Sⓞⓞ-VRⓤ

No, thank you.

Non, merci.

NⓄⓝ MⒺR-SⒺⒺ

I'm just looking.

Je regarde seulement.

ZH(uh) R(uh)-G(ah)RD S(ou)L-M(ah)ñ

It's very expensive.

C'est trop cher.

S(A) TR(O) SH(ê)R

Can't you give me a discount?

Pouvez-vous me donner un prix réduit?

P(oo)-V(A) V(oo) M(uh) D(O)-N(A) (uh)ñ

PR(EE) R(A)-DW(EE)

I'll take it!

Je le prendrai!

ZH(uh) L(uh) PR(ah)ñ-DR(A)

I'd like a receipt please.

Je voudrais un reçu.

ZH(uh) V(oo)-DR(A) (uh)ñ R(uh)-S(ew)

I want to return this.

Je voudrais rendre ceci.

ZH(uh) V(oo)-DR(A) R(ah)ñ-DR(uh) S(uh)-S(EE)

It doesn't fit.

Ça ne va pas.

S(ah) N(uh) V(ah) P(ah)

PHRASEMAKER

I'm looking for…
Je cherche...
ZH@ SH@RSH…

▸ **a bakery**
une boulangerie
@N B@-L@ñ-ZH@-R@

▸ **a bank**
une banque
@N B@NK

▸ **a barber**
un coiffeur
@ñ KW@-F@R

▸ **a camera shop**
un magasin de photo
@ñ M@-G@-S@ñ D@ F@-T@

▸ **a hair dresser**
un coiffeur
@ñ KW@-F@R

▸ **a pharmacy**
une pharmacie
@N F@R-M@-S@

PHRASEMAKER

Do you sell...

Est-ce que vous vendez...

ĕS-Kᵘʰ Vᵒᵒ Vₐʰñ-DⒶ...

▸ **aspirin?**

l'aspirine?

LₐʰS-PⒺⒺ-ℝⒺⒺN

▸ **cigarettes?**

les cigarettes?

LⒶ SⒺⒺ-Gₐʰ-ℝĕT

▸ **deodorant?**

le deodorant?

Lᵘʰ DⒶ-Ⓞ-DⓄ-ℝₐʰñ

▸ **dresses?**

les robes?

LⒶ ℝⓄB

▸ **film?**

la pellicule?

Lₐʰ Pĕ-LⒺⒺ-KᵉʷL

▶ **pantyhose?**
le collant?

L@h KO-L@hñ

▶ **perfume?**
le parfum?

L@h P@hR-F@hñ

▶ **razor blades?**
les lames de rasoir?

L@ L@hM D@h R@h-SW@hR

▶ **shampoo?**
le shampooing?

L@h SH@hM-P@@-@@N

▶ **shaving cream?**
la crème à raser?

L@h KR@M @h R@h-S@

▶ **shirts?**
les chemises?

L@ SH@h-M@@Z

▶ **soap?**
le savon?

L@h S@h-VOñ

▸ **sunglasses?**

les lunettes de soleil?

L Ⓐ Lⓔⓦ-Nⓔ̈T Dⓤⓗ SⓄ-LⒶ

▸ **sunscreen?**

la crème solaire?

L ⓐⓗ KRⒷⓔ̈M SⓄ-Lⓔ̈R

▸ **toothbrushes?**

les brosses à dents?

L Ⓐ BRⓄ <u>S</u>ⓐⓗ Dⓐⓗñ

▸ **toothpaste?**

le dentifrice?

L ⓤⓗ Dⓐⓗñ-TⒺⒺ-FRⒺⒺS

▸ **water?**

l'eau nature?

L Ⓞ Nⓐⓗ-TⓔⓦR

▸ **water?** (mineral)

l'eau minérale?

L Ⓞ MⒺⒺ-NⒶ-RⓐⓗL

ESSENTIAL SERVICES

THE BANK

As a traveler in a foreign country your primary contact with banks will be to exchange money. Keep in mind that many banks close on Monday and Saturday afternoon.

- The French national currency is the Euro (formerly French franc). Bank notes are in denominations of € 500, 200, 100, 50, 20, 10 and 5. Coins are in denominations of 2 and 1 €, and 50, 20, 10, 5, 2, and 1 € cents.

- Change enough funds before leaving home to pay for tips, food, and transportation to your final destination.

- Generally, you will receive a better rate of exchange at a bank than at a Bureau de Change or at the airport.

- Current exchange rates are posted in banks and published daily in city newspapers.

- ATM machines are readily available in large cities like Paris as well as smaller towns, and credit cards are accepted.

KEY WORDS

Bank

La banque

L@ B@NK

Exchange office

Le bureau de change

L@ B@-R@ D@ SH@ñZH

Money

L'argent

L@B-ZH@ñ

Money order

Le mandat-poste

L@ M@ñ-D@ P@ST

Travelers' checks

Les chèques de voyage

L@ SH@K D@ VW@-Y@ZH

USEFUL PHRASES

Where is the bank?

Où est la banque?

ⓞⓞ Ⓐ Lⓐⓗ BⓐⓗNK

What time does the bank open?

A quelle heure est-ce que la banque s'ouvre?

ⓐⓗ Kⓔ LⓞⓤR ⓔS-Kⓤⓗ
Lⓐⓗ BⓐⓗNK Sⓞⓞ-VRⓤⓗ

Where is the exchange office?

Où est le bureau de change?

ⓞⓞ Ⓐ Lⓤⓗ Bⓔⓦ-Rⓞ Dⓤⓗ SHⓐⓗñZH

What time does the exchange office open?

A quelle heure s'ouvre le bureau de change?

ⓐⓗ Kⓔ LⓞⓤR Sⓞⓞ-VRⓤⓗ Lⓤⓗ
Bⓔⓦ-Rⓞ Dⓤⓗ SHⓐⓗñZH

Can I change dollars here?

Puis-je changer des dollars ici?

PWⓔⓔ-ZHⓤⓗ SHⓐⓗñ-ZHⒶ DⒶ
Dⓞ-LⓐⓗR ⓔⓔ-Sⓔⓔ

Can you change this?

Pouvez-vous changer ceci?

P㏄-V④ V㏄ SH⒜ñ-ZH④ S⒰-S㋞

What is the exchange rate?

Quel est le taux de change?

K⒠ L̲④ L⒰ T◎ D⒰ SH⒜ñZH

I would like large bills.

Je voudrais de grands billets.

ZH⒰ V㏄-DR④ D⒰
GR⒜ñ B㋞-Y④

I would like small bills.

Je voudrais de petits billets.

ZH⒰ V㏄-DR④ D⒰ P⒰-T㋞ B㋞-Y④

I need change.

J'ai besoin de monnaie.

ZH④ B⒰-ZW⒜ñ D⒰ M◎-N④

Do you have an ATM?

Avez-vous un GAB?

⒜-V④ V㏄ ⒰ñ ZH④ ⒜ B④

POST OFFICE

PTT and **POSTE** identify the post office. Stamps can be purchased at a **Bureau de Tabac**, as well as at certain cafés and in post offices.

KEY WORDS

Airmail

Par avion

P(ah)R (ah)-V(EE)-(O)ñ

Letter

La lettre

L(ah) L(ĕ)-TR(uh)

Post office

La poste

L(ah) P(O)ST

Postcard

La carte postale

L(ah) K(ah)RT P(O)S-T(ah)L

Stamp

Le timbre

L(uh) T(ah)ñ-BR(uh)

USEFUL PHRASES

Where is the post office?

Où est la poste?

ⓞⓞ Ⓐ Lⓐⓗ PⓞST

What time does the post office open?

A quelle heure est-ce que la poste s'ouvre?

ⓐⓗ Kⓔ̈ LⓞⓤⒷ ⒠S-Kⓤⓗ Lⓐⓗ
PⓞST Sⓞⓞ-VⒷⓤⓗ

I need stamps.

J'ai besoin de timbres.

ZHⒶ Bⓤⓗ-ZWⓐⓗñ Dⓤⓗ Tⓐⓗñ-BⒷⓤⓗ

I need an envelope.

J'ai besoin d'une enveloppe.

ZHⒶ Bⓤⓗ-ZWⓐⓗñ DⓔⓦN
ⓐⓗñ-Vⓔ̈-LⓞP

I need a pen.

J'ai besoin d'un stylo.

ZHⒶ Bⓤⓗ-ZWⓐⓗñ Dⓤⓗñ STⒺⒺ-Lⓞ

TELEPHONE

Placing phone calls in a foreign country can be a test of will and stamina! Besides the obvious language barriers, service can vary greatly from one town to the next.

- In France, phone calls can be made from the post office, Métro station, and most cafés with phone cards, **télécartes**.

- Coin operated booths still exist; however, they are often difficult to find. If you plan to make frequent use of the French phone system, it is best to purchase a **télécarte** as soon as possible.

- You can purchase a telephone card at tobacconists, post offices, and approved sales points which display the poster **TELECARTE EN VENTE ICI**. These cards allow you to easily make calls in most phone booths in France.

KEY WORDS

Information

Les renseignements

L@ Rah̃-S̄eN-Y@-M@ñ

Long distance

De communication interurbaine

D@ K⊙-M@-N€€-K@-S€€-O̅ñ

@ñ-T̄eR-@R-B̄eN

Operator

Le standardiste

L@ ST@N-D@R-D€€ST

Phone book

L'annuaire

L@-N@-@R

Public telephone

Le téléphone public

L@ T@-L@-F⊙N P@-BL€€K

Telephone

Le téléphone

L@ T@-L@-F⊙N

USEFUL PHRASES

May I use your telephone?

Puis-je me servir de votre téléphone?

PW(EE)-ZH(uh) M(uh) S(ĕ)R-V(EE)R D(uh)
V(O)-TR(uh) T(A)-L(A)-F(O)N

Operator, I don't speak French.

Madame (f) (monsieur) (m)
le standardiste, je ne parle pas français.

M(ă)-D(ă)M (M(uh)-SY(ou))
L(uh) ST(ah)N-D(ah)R-D(EE)ST ZH(uh)N-(uh)
P(ah)RL P(ah) FR(ah)ñ-S(A)

I would like to make a long-distance call.

Je voudrais faire un appel au longue distance.

ZH(uh) V(oo)-DR(A) F(ĕ)R (uh)ñ (ă)-P(ĕ)L
L(ah)NG D(EE)S-T(ah)NS

I would like to make a call to the United States.

Je voudrais faire un appel aux Etats-Unis.

ZH(uh) V(oo)-DR(A) F(ĕ)R (uh)ñ (ă)-P(ĕ)L
(O) Z(A)-T(ah) Z(ew)-N(EE)

I want to call…

Je voudrais téléphoner...

ZHᵘʰ Vᵒᵒ-DRⒶ TⒶ-LⒶ-Fⓞ-NⒶ...

SIGHTSEEING AND ENTERTAINMENT

In most towns in France you will find tourist information offices. Here you can usually obtain brochures, maps, historical information, bus and train schedules.

Lively places, an abundance of atmosphere, shopping, festivals, great food, and fine wine invite travelers to experience all that France has to offer.

PARIS SIGHTS

L'Arc de Triomphe
LⓐRK Dⓤh TRⒺⒺ-ⓄñF

Le Louvre
Lⓤh LⓄⓄ-VRⓤh

La Tour Eiffel
Lⓐh TⓄⓄR ⒺⒺ-FⓔL

Notre Dame
NⓄ-TRⓤh DⓐhM

Les Champs-Elysées
LⒶ SHⓐhñ-ZⒶ-LⒺⒺ-ZⒶ

KEY WORDS

Admission

L'entrée

Map

Le plan

L⒰ PL⒜ñ

Reservation

La réservation

L⒜ R⒜-S⒠R-V⒜-S⒠-O⒩

Ticket

Le ticket

Tour

La visite

L⒜ V⒠-Z⒠T

Tour guide

Le guide

USEFUL PHRASES

Where is the tourist office?

Où est l'office de tourisme?

ⓞⓞ Ⓐ LⓄ-FⒺⒺS Dⓤⓗ
TⓞⓞR-ⒺⒺZ-Mⓐⓗ

Is there a tour to…?

Y a-t-il une visite guidée à…?

ⒺⒺ ⓐⓗ-TⒺⒺL ⓔⓦN VⒺⒺ-ZⒺⒺT
GⒺⒺ-D(Ⓐ) ⓐⓗ…

Where do I buy a ticket?

Où puis-je acheter un ticket?

ⓞⓞ PWⒺⒺ-ZHⓤⓗ ⓐⓗSH-TⒶ
ⓤⓗñ TⒺⒺ-KⒶ

How much does the tour cost?

Combien coûte la visite?

KⓄñ-BⒺⒺ-ⓐⓗñ KⓞⓞT Lⓐⓗ VⒺⒺ-ZⒺⒺT

How long does the tour take?

La visite prend combien de temps?

Lⓐⓗ VⒺⒺ-ZⒺⒺT PRⓐⓗñ
KⓄñ-BⒺⒺ-ⓐⓗñ Dⓤⓗ Tⓐⓗñ

Does the guide speak English?

Est-ce que le guide parle anglais?

ⓔS-Kⓤⓗ Lⓤⓗ GⒺⒺD PⓐⓗRL ⓐⓗñ-GLⒶ

Do children pay?

Les enfant paient?

LⒶ Zⓐⓗñ-Fⓐⓗñ PⒶ

What time does the show start?

A quelle heure commence le spectacle?

ⓐⓗ Kⓔ LⓞⓤR Kⓞ-MⓐⓗñS
Lⓤⓗ SPⓔK-TⓐKL

Do I need reservations?

Il faut avoir des réservations?

ⒺⒺL Fⓞ Tⓐⓗ-VWⓐⓗR DⒶ
RⒶ-SⓔR-Vⓐⓗ-SⒺⒺ-Oñ

Where can we go dancing?

Où est-ce qu'on peut danser?

ⓞⓞ ⓔS KⓞN Pⓞⓤ Dⓐⓗñ-SⒶ

Is there a cover charge?

Est-ce que l'entrée est payante?

ⓔS-Kⓤⓗ LⓐⓗN-TRⒶ PⒶ-ⓐⓗNT

PHRASEMAKER

May I invite you...

Je vous invite...

ZH⒰ V⓪ Zⓐ̃-V⒠T...

▸ **to a concert?**

à un concert?

⒜ ⒰̃ K⓪̃-S⒠R

▸ **to dance?**

à danser?

⒜ D⒜̃-S⒜

▸ **to dinner?**

au dîner?

⓪ D⒠-N⒜

▸ **to the movies?**

au cinéma?

⓪ S⒠-N⒜-M⒜

▸ **to the theater?**

au théâtre?

⓪ T⒜-⒜-TR⒰

PHRASEMAKER

Where can I find...

Où se trouve...

⊚ Sⓤⓗ TRⓞⓞV...

▶ **a health club?**

un centre sportif?

ⓤⓗñ Sⓐⓗñ-TRⓤⓗ SPⓞB-TⓔⓔF

▶ **a swimming pool?**

une piscine?

ⓔⓦN Pⓔⓔ-SⓔⓔN

▶ **a tennis court?**

un terrain de tennis?

ⓤⓗñ Tⓔ-Bⓐñ Dⓤⓗ Tⓔ-NⓔⓔS

▶ **a golf course?**

un terrain de golf?

ⓤⓗñ Tⓔ-Bⓐñ Dⓤⓗ GⓞLF

HEALTH

Hopefully you will not need
medical attention on your trip.
If you do, it is important to
communicate basic information
regarding your condition.

- Check with your insurance company before
  leaving home to find out if you are covered in
  a foreign country. You may want to purchase
  traveler's insurance before leaving home.

- If you take prescription medicine, carry your
  prescription with you. Have your prescriptions
  translated before you leave home.

- Take a small first-aid kit with you.

- Your embassy or consulate should be able to
  assist you in finding health care.

- A GREEN CROSS indicates a pharmacy,
  where minor treatment can be handled by the
  pharmacist.

- **Droguerie** is similar to a drugstore but also
  sells household goods and toiletries.

- {H} indicates **l'hôpital** (hospital)

KEY WORDS

Ambulance

L'ambulance

L@ñ-B@w-L@ñS

Dentist

Le dentiste

L@ D@ñ-T@ST

Doctor

Le médecin

L@ M@-D@-S@ñ

Emergency

L'urgence

L@B-ZH@ñS

Hospital

L'hôpital

L@-P@-T@L

Prescription

La prescription

L@ PR@-SKR@P-S@-O@ñ

USEFUL PHRASES

I am sick.

Je suis malade.

ZH⓾ SW㊙ M⒜-L⒜D

I need a doctor.

J'ai besoin d'un docteur.

ZH④ B⓾-ZW⒜ñ D⓾ñ D⒜K-T㋾B

It's an emergency!

C'est une urgence!

S④ T㋎ N㋎B-ZH⒜ñS

Where is the nearest hospital?

Où est l'hôpital le plus proche?

㋡ ④ L⓪-P㊙-T⒜L

L⓾ PL㋎ PB⒜SH

Call an ambulance!

Faites venir une ambulance!

F㋏T V⓾-N㊙B ㋎ N⒜ñ-B㋎-L⒜ñS

I'm allergic to…

Je suis allergique à...

ZH⓪ SW㋐ Z̲⓪-L㋐B-ZH㋐ K̲⓪...

I'm pregnant.

Je suis enceinte.

ZH⓪ SW㋐ Z̲⓪ñ-S㋐ñT

I'm diabetic.

Je suis diabétique.

ZH⓪ SW㋐ D㋐-⓪-B㋐-T㋐K

I have a heart problem.

J'ai un problème cardiaque.

ZH④ ⓪N PB⓪-BL㋐M K⓪B-D㋐-④K

I have high blood pressure.

Je fais de l'hypertension.

ZH⓪ F④ D⓪
L㋐-P㋐B-T⓪ñ-S㋐-Oñ

I have low blood pressure.

Je fais de l'hypotension.

ZH⓪ F④ D⓪
L㋐-PO-T⓪ñ-S㋐-Oñ

PHRASEMAKER

I need...

J'ai besoin...

ZH𝖠 B𝗎𝗁-ZW𝖺ñ...

▶ **a doctor**

d'un docteur

D𝗎𝗁ñ D𝖺K-T𝗈𝗎R

▶ **a dentist**

d'un dentiste

D𝗎𝗁ñ D𝖺ñ-T𝖤𝖤ST

▶ **a nurse**

d'une infirmière

D𝖾𝗐 N𝖺ñ-F𝖤𝖤R-M𝖤𝖤-ĕR

▶ **an optician**

d'un opticien

D𝗎𝗁ñ NOP-T𝖤𝖤-S𝖤𝖤-𝖺ñ

▶ **a pharmacist**

d'un pharmacien

D𝗎𝗁ñ F𝖺R-M𝖺h-S𝖤𝖤-𝖺ñ

PHRASEMAKER

(AT THE PHARMACY)

Do you have...

Avez-vous..

ⓐⓗ-Vⓐ Vⓞⓞ...

▸ **aspirin?**

de l'aspirine?

Dⓤⓗ LⓐⓗS-Pⓔⓔ-RⓔⓔN

▸ **Band-Aids?**

des bandages?

Dⓐ Bⓐⓗñ-DⓐⓗZH

▸ **cough medicine?**

le sirop contre la toux?

Lⓤⓗ Sⓔⓔ-Rⓞ Kⓞñ-TRⓤⓗ Lⓐⓗ Tⓞⓞ

▸ **ear drops?**

les gouttes pour les oreilles?

Lⓐ GⓞⓞT PⓞⓞR Lⓐ Zⓞ-Rⓐ-Yⓞⓤ

▸ **eyedrops?**

les gouttes pour les yeux?

Lⓐ GⓞⓞT PⓞⓞR Lⓐ Zⓔⓔ-Yⓞⓤ

BUSINESS TRAVEL

It is important to show appreciation and interest in another person's language and culture, particularly when doing business. A few well-pronounced phrases can make a great impression.

I have an appointment.

J'ai rendez-vous.

ZH④ R⑨ñ-D④-V⑳

Here is my card.

Voici ma carte.

VW⑨-S㏄ M⑨ K⑨RT

May I speak to Mr…?

Puis-je parler à Monsieur…?

PW㏄-ZH⑩ P⑨R-L④ ⑨ M⑩-SY⑳…

May I speak to Mrs…?

Puis-je parler à Madame…?

PW㏄-ZH⑩ P⑨R-L④ ⑨ M⑨-D⑨M…

I need an interpreter.

J'ai besoin d'un interprète.

ZH④ B⑩-ZW⑨ñ D⑩ñ
N⑨ñ-T㏄R-PR㏄T

KEY WORDS

Appointment

Le rendez-vous

L⓾ Rⓐñ-Dⓐ-V⓸

Meeting

La réunion

Lⓐ Rⓐ-⓮N-Yⓞñ

Marketing

Le marketing

L⓾ MⓐR-Kⓔ̃-Tⓔ⓮N

Presentation

La présentation

Lⓐ PRⓐ-Sⓔ̃N-Tⓐ-Sⓔ⓮-Ⓞñ

Sales

Les ventes

Lⓐ VⓐñT

PHRASEMAKER

I need…

J'ai besoin...

ZH④ B⑩-ZW⑩ñ…

▶ **a computer**

d'un ordinateur

D⑩ñ N⑩R-D㋐-N⑩-T⑩R

▶ **a copy machine**

d'un copieur

D⑩ñ K⑩-P㋐-⑩R

▶ **a conference room**

d'une salle de conférences

D㋐N S⑩L D⑩ K⑩ñ-F④-R⑩ñS

▶ **a fax machine**

d'un télécopieur

D⑩ñ T④-L④-K⑩-P㋐-⑩R

▶ **an interpreter**

d'un interprète

D⑩ñ N⑩ñ-T㋐R-PR㋐T

▶ **a lawyer**

d'un avocat

Dⓤⓗñ Nⓐⓗ-Vⓞ-Kⓐⓗ

▶ **a notary**

d'un notaire

Dⓤⓗñ Nⓞ-Tⓔⓡ

▶ **overnight delivery**

de livraison exprès

Dⓤⓗ Lⓔⓔ-Vⓡⓐ-Sⓞñ ⓔKS-Pⓡⓔ

▶ **paper**

de papier

Dⓤⓗ Pⓐⓗ-Pⓔⓔ-Ⓐ

▶ **a pen**

d'un stylo

Dⓤⓗñ STⓔⓔ-Lⓞ

▶ **a pencil**

d'un crayon

Dⓤⓗñ KⓡⒶ-Ⓞñ

▶ **a secretary**

d'un secrétaire

Dⓤⓗñ Sⓔ-Kⓡⓔ-Tⓔⓡ

GENERAL INFORMATION

From cool summers in the west to hot summers and very cold winters in central and eastern France, there is something for everyone!

SEASONS

Spring

Le printemps

Luh PRañ-Tañ

Summer

L'été

LA-TA

Autumn

L'automne

LO-Tuhñ

Winter

L'hiver

LEE-VëR

THE DAYS

Monday
lundi

Luhñ-DEE

Tuesday
mardi

Mah'R-DEE

Wednesday
mercredi

MẽR-KRuh-DEE

Thursday
jeudi

ZHou-DEE

Friday
vendredi

Vahñ-DRuh-DEE

Saturday
samedi

Sah'M-DEE

Sunday
dimanche

DEE-Mah'ñSH

THE MONTHS

January	February
janvier	février
ZHⓐñ-Vⓔⓔ-Ⓐ	FⒶ-VRⓔⓔ-Ⓐ

March	April
mars	avril
MⓐBS	ⓐV-RⓔⓔL

May	June
mai	juin
MⒶ	ZHⓞⓞ-ⓐñ

July	August
juillet	août
ZHWⓔⓔ-Ⓐ	ⓞⓞT

September	October
septembre	octobre
SⓔP-Tⓐñ-BRⓤⓗ	ⓐK-TⓄ-BRⓤⓗ

November	December
novembre	décembre
NⓄ-Vⓐñ-BRⓤⓗ	DⒶ-Sⓐñ-BRⓤⓗ

COLORS

Black	**White**
Noir (m) / Noire (f)	Blanc (m) / Blanche (f)
NW@B	BL@ñ / BL@ñSH
Blue	**Brown**
Bleu (m) / Bleue (f)	Brun (m) / Brune (f)
BL@	BR@ñ / BR@N
Gray	**Gold**
Gris (m) / Grise (f)	Or
GR@ / GR@S	@B
Orange	**Yellow**
Orange	Jaune
@-B@ñZH	ZH@N
Red	**Green**
Rouge	Vert (m) / Verte (f)
R@ZH	V@B / V@BT
Pink	**Purple**
Rose	Violet (m) / Violette (f)
R@Z	V@-@-L@ / V@-@-L@T

NUMBERS

0	1	2
Zéro	Un	Deux
ZA-RO	uhñ	Dou

3	4	5
Trois	Quatre	Cinq
TRWah	Ka-TRuh	SaNK

6	7	8
Six	Sept	Huit
SEES	SeT	WEET

9	10	11
Neuf	Dix	Onze
NouF	DEES	OñZ

12	13	14
Douze	Treize	Quatorze
DooZ	TReZ	Ka-TORZ

15	16	17
Quinze	Seize	Dix-sept
KañZ	SeZ	DEE-SeT

18	19	
Dix-huit	Dix-neuf	
DEEZ-WEET	DEEZ-NouF	

20	**30**
Vingt	Trente
Vãñ	TR@ñT

40	**50**
Quarante	Cinquante
Kẽ-R@ñT	Sãñ-K@ñT

60	**70**
Soixante	Soixante-dix
SW@-Z@ñT	SW@-Z@ñT D€S

80	**90**
Quatre-vingt	Quatre-vingt-dix
Kã-TR@ V@ñ	Kã-TR@ V@ñ D€S

100	**1000**
Cent	Mille
S@ñ	M€L

1,000,000
Million
M€-L€-Oñ

FRENCH VERBS

Verbs are the action words of any language. In French there are three main types; **–er**, **–ir**, and **–re**.

The foundation form for all verbs is called the infinitive. This is the form you will find in dictionaries. In English, we place "to" in front of the verb name to give us the infinitive; e.g., to speak. In French, **l'infinitif** is one word, **parler**, and means by itself to speak, and (as in English) it does not change its form.

On the following pages you will see the present tense conjugation of the three regular verb groups: **–er**, **–ir**, and **–re**. Conjugating a verb is what you do naturally in your own language: *I speak, he finishes, they sell.* A verb is called regular when it follows one of these three models: its basic form does not change, just the endings that correspond to the subject of the verb.

In your study of French, you will come across irregular verbs and verbs with spelling changes. Their conjugation will require memorization. However, the Phrasemaker on page 128 will help you avoid this problem. First choose a form of "want," then select an infinitive; 150 are provided in the following section. And because the infintive does not change, you don't need to worry about the conjugation of the verb or whether it is regular or irregular!

–ER VERB CONJUGATION

Find below the present tense conjugation for the regular
–ER verb **parler**, meaning **to speak**. The English equivalent
is: *I speak* (or *I am speaking*), *you speak* (*you are
speaking*), etc. For regular **–ER** verbs like this, drop the
infinitive ending and add **-e**, **-es**, **-e**, **-ons**, **-ez** or **-ent**.

I speak.

Je parl**e**.

ZH⓾ PⓐRL

You speak. (informal)

Tu parl**es**.

T⓪⓪ PⓐRL

He speaks. / She speaks. / (One) speaks.

Il / Elle / On parl**e**.

ⒺⒺL / ⒠L / ⓐñ PⓐRL

We speak.

Nous parl**ons**.

N⓪⓪ PⓐR-L⓪ñ

You speak. (plural)

Vous parl**ez**.

V⓪⓪ PⓐR-LⒶ

They speak.

Ils / Elles parl**ent**.

ⒺⒺL / ⒠L PⓐR-Lⓐñ

–IR VERB CONJUGATION

Find below the present tense conjugation for the regular **–IR** verb **finir**, meaning *to* finish. The English equivalent is: *I finish* (or *I am finishing*), *you finish* (*you are finishing*), etc. For regular **–IR** verbs like this, drop the infinitive ending and add **-is**, **-is**, **-it**, **-issons**, **-issez** or **-issent**.

I finish.

Je fin**is**.

ZH⒰ F㋐-N㋐

You finish. (informal)

Tu fin**is**.

T⒪⒪ F㋐-N㋐

He finishes. / She finishes. / (One) finishes.

Il / Elle / On fin**it**.

㋐L / ⒠L / ⒜ⓗñ F㋐-N㋐T

We finish.

Nous fin**issons**.

N⒪⒪ F㋐-N㋐-S⒪ñ

You finish. (plural; formal singular)

Vous fin**issez**.

V⒪⒪ F㋐-N㋐-Z⒜

They finish.

Ils / Elles fin**issent**.

㋐L / ⒠L F㋐-N㋐-S⒜ⓗñ

–RE VERB CONJUGATION

Find below the present tense conjugation for the regular **–RE** verb **vendre**, meaning *to sell*. The English equivalent is: *I sell* (or *I am selling*), *you sell* (*you are selling*), etc. For regular **–RE** verbs like this, drop the infinitive ending and add **-s**, **-s**, **-** , **-ons**, **-ez** or **-ent**.

I sell.

Je vend**s**.

ZH⓪ V⑨ñ

You sell. (informal)

Tu vend**s**.

T⑩ V⑨ñ

He sells. / She sells. / (One) sells.

Il / Elle / On vend.

⑤L / ⑥L / ⑨ñ V⑨ñ

We sell.

Nous vend**ons**.

N⑩ V⑨N-D⑨ñ

You sell. (plural; formal singular)

Vous par**lez**.

V⑩ V⑨ñ-D⑤

They sell.

Ils / Elles vend**ent**.

⑤L / ⑥L V⑨N-D⑨ñ

PHRASEMAKER

I want...

Je veux...

ZH⒰ V⒪...

You want...

Tu veux... (informal)

T⒪ V⒪...

Vous voulez... (formal)

V⒪ V⒪-L⒜...

It is easy to recognize French verbs in their infinitive form because they always end in **-er**, **-ir**, or **-re**!

He wants...   ◀

Il veut...

⒠L V⒪...

▶ **to speak**

parl**er**

P⒜R-L⒜

She wants...   ◀

Elle veut...

⒠L V⒪...

▶ **to finish**

fin**ir**

F⒠-N⒠R

We want...   ◀

Nous voulons...

N⒪ V⒪-L⒪ñ...

▶ **to sell**

vend**re**

V⒜N-DR⒰

They want...

Ils veulent...

⒠L V⒪L...

150 VERBS

Here are some essential verbs that will carry you a long way towards learning French with the EPLS Vowel Symbol System!

to add

ajouter

@h-ZH@@-T@

to allow

permettre

P@B-M@T-TB@h

to answer

répondre

B@-P@N-DB@h

to arrive

arriver

@h-B@@-V@

to ask

demander

D@h-M@ñ-D@

to attack

attaquer

@h-T@h-K@

to attend

assister

@h-S@@S-T@

to be

être

@-TB@h

to be able

pouvoir

P@@-VW@B

to beg

mendier

M@ñ-D@@-@

to begin

commencer

K@-M@ñ-S@

to bother (annoy)

embêter

@M-B@h-T@

129

to break
briser
BR㋐-Z㋐

to breathe
respirer
R㋐-SP㋐-R㋐

to bring
apporter
㋐P-P㋐R-T㋐

to build
construire
K㋐N-STR㋐-㋐R

to burn
brûler
BR㋐-L㋐

to buy
acheter
㋐SH-T㋐

to call
appeler
㋐P-L㋐

to cancel
annuler
㋐N-Y㋐-L㋐

to change
changer
SH㋐ñ-ZH㋐

to chew
mâcher
M㋐-SH㋐

to clean
nettoyer
N㋐T-TW㋐-Y㋐

to climb
monter
M㋐N-T㋐

to close
fermer
F㋐R-M㋐

to come
venir
V㋐-N㋐R

to cook

cuisiner

KWEE-ZEE-NA

to contact

contacter

KON-TAK-TA

to count

compter

KOMP-TA

to cry

pleurer

PLOU-RA

to cut

couper

KOO-PA

to dance

danser

DAHÑ-SA

to decide

décider

DEE-SEE-DA

to declare

déclarer

DEE-KLAH-RA

to depart

partir

PAHR-TEER

disturb

déranger

DÉ-RAHÑ-ZHA

to do

faire

FÉR

to drink

boire

BWAHR

to dry

sécher

SÉ-SHA

to earn

gagner

GÃN-YA

to eat
manger
M@ñ-ZH@

to enjoy
aimer
@-M@

to enter
entrer
@ñ-TR@

to entertain
divertir
D@-V@r-T@R

to envy
envier
@ñ-V@-@

to explain
expliquer
@KS-PL@-K@

to feel
sentir
S@ñ-T@R

to fight
lutter
L@T-T@

to fill
remplir
R@M-PL@R

to find
trouver
TR@-V@

to finish
finir
F@-N@R

to fix
fixer
F@K-S@

to flirt
flirter
FL@R-T@

to fly
voler
V@-L@

to forget	to have
oublier	avoir
ⓄⓄB-Lⓔⓔ-Ⓐ	ⓐⓗV-WⓐⓗR

to forgive	to hear
pardonner	entendre
PⓐⓗR-DⓄN-NⒶ	ⓐⓗñ-Tⓐⓗñ-DRⓤⓗ

to get	to help
obtenir	aider
ⓄB-Tⓔ̃-NⓔⓔR	Ⓐ-DⒶ

to give	to hide
donner	cacher
DⓄN-NⒶ	Kⓐⓗ-SHⒶ

to go	to hold
aller	tenir
ⓐⓗ-LⒶ	Tⓔ̃-NⓔⓔR

to greet	to imagine
saluer	imaginer
Sⓐ̃L-ⓄⓄ-Ⓐ	ⓔⓔ-Mⓐⓗ-ZHⓔⓔ-NⒶ

to happen	to inhale
se passer	aspirer
Sⓔ̃ PⓐⓗS-SⒶ	ⓐⓗS-Pⓔⓔ-RⒶ

to judge

juger

ZH⊚-ZH🅐

to jump

sauter

S⊙-T🅐

to kiss

embrasser

🅐ñ-BR🅐-Sẽ

to know (knowledge)

savoir

S🅐-VW🅐R

to know (person)

connaître

K⊙-Nẽ-TR🅔🅦

to laugh

rire

R🅔🅔-R🅤🅗

to learn

apprendre

🅐P-PR🅐ñ-DR🅤🅗

to leave

quitter

K🅔🅔T-T🅐

to lie (not the truth)

mentir

M🅐ñ-T🅔🅔R

to lift

lever

L⊚-V🅐

to listen

écouter

🅐-K⊚-T🅐

to live

vivre

V🅔🅔-VR🅤🅗

to look

regarder

Rẽ-G🅐R-D🅐

to lose

perdre

PẽR-DR🅤🅗

to love

aimer

Ⓐ-MⒶ

to make

faire

FⒺR

to marry

marier

Mⓐⱨ-Rㅌㅌ-Ⓐ

to measure

mesurer

MⒺ-Zⓞⓤ-RⒶ

to miss

manquer

Mⓐⱨñ-KⒶ

to move

déplacer

DⒶ-PLⓐⱨ-SⒶ

to need (require)

nécessiter

NⒺ-SⒺ-Sㅌㅌ-TⒶ

to notify

aviser

ⓐ̃-Vㅌㅌ-ZⒶ

to offer

offrir

ⓄF-FRㅌㅌR

to open

ouvrir

ⓞⓞ-VRㅌㅌ'R

to order

commander

KⓄ-MⓐⱨN-DⒶ

to pack

emballer

ⓐⱨM-BⓐⱨL-LⒶ

to paint

peindre

Pⓐ̃ñ-DRⓤⱨ

to pass

passer

PⓐⱨS-SⒶ

to pay (for)

payer

Pĕ-YⒶ

to play

jouer

ZHoo-Ⓐ

to pretend

prétendre

PRĕ-Tahñ-DRuh

to print

imprimer

ahM-PREE-MⒶ

to promise

promettre

PRO-MĕT-TRuh

to pronounce

prononcer

PRO-Nuhn-SⒶ

to push

pousser

Poo-S-SⒶ

to put

mettre

MĕT-TRuh

to quit

quitter

KEE-TⒶ

to read

lire

LEE-Ruh

to recomend

recommander

Ruh-KO-Mahñ-DⒶ

to rent

louer

Loo-Ⓐ

to remember

rappeler

Rah-PLⒶ

to rescue

sauver

SO-VⒶ

to rest	**to show**
reposer	montrer
Ruh-PO-ZA	MOñ-TRA
to return	**to sign**
retourner	signer
Ruh-TOR-NA	SEEN-YA
to run	**to sing**
courir	chanter
Koo-REER	SHahñ-TA
to say	**to sit**
dire	s'asseoir
DEE-Ruh	Suh-SWahR
to see	**to sleep**
voir	dormir
VWahR	DOR-MEER
to sell	**to smoke**
vendre	fumer
Vahñ-DRuh	Few-MA
to send	**to smile**
envoyer	sourire
ahN-Voy-YA	Soo-REE-Ruh

to speak

parler

P@B-L@

to spell

épeler

@-PL@

to spend (money)

dépenser

D@-P@ñ-S@

to start (begin)

commencer

K@-M@ñ-S@

to stay

rester

B@-ST@

to stop

arrêter

@-B@-T@

to study

étudier

@-T@-D@-@

to swim

nager

N@-ZH@

to take

prendre

PB@ñ-DB@

to talk

parler

P@B-L@

to teach

enseigner

@ñ-S@N-Y@

to tell

raconter

B@-K@ñ-T@

to touch

toucher

T@-SH@

to think

penser

P@ñ-S@

to travel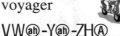
voyager
VW@h-Y@h-ZH@

to try
essayer
@S-S@-Y@

to understand
comprendre
K@M-PR@h@ñ-DR@h

to use
utiliser
@-T@E-L@E-Z@

to visit
visiter
V@E-Z@E-T@

to wait
attendre
@hT-T@hñ-DR@h

to walk
marcher
M@hR-SH@

to want
vouloir
V@L-W@hR

to wash
laver
L@h-V@

to watch
regarder
R@h-G@hR-D@

to win
gagner
G@hN-Y@

to work
travailler
TR@h-V@I-Y@

to worry
inquiéter
@hñ-K@E-T@

to write
écrire
@-KR@E-R@h

DICTIONARY

Each English entry is followed by the French word and then the EPLS Vowel Symbol System. French nouns are either masculine or feminine. The French article **le** precedes masculine nouns and **la** precedes feminine nouns in the singular form. **Les** indicates feminine or masculine plural. In some cases, masculine and feminine are indicated by (m) and (f) respectively.

A

a / an un (m) ⓤñ   une (f) ⓔⓦN

a lot beaucoup Bⓞ-Kⓞⓞ

able (to be) pouvoir Pⓞⓞ-VWⓐⓑR

above au dessus (de) ⓞ Dⓤⓗ-Sⓔⓦ (Dⓤⓗ)

accident l'accident (m) LⓐⓗK-Sⓔⓔ-Dⓐⓗñ

accommodation le logement Lⓤⓗ LⓞZH-Mⓐⓗñ

account le compte Lⓤⓗ KⓞñT

address l'adresse (f) Lⓐⓗ-DRⓔ̃S

admission l'entrée (f) Lⓐⓗñ-TRⓐ

afraid (to be) avoir peur ⓐⓗ-VWⓐⓗR PⓞⓤR

after après ⓐⓗ-PRⓐ

afternoon l'après-midi (m) Lⓐⓗ-PRⓐ Mⓔⓔ-Dⓔⓔ

---

air conditioning d'air climatisé (m)

    DĕR KLEE-Mah-TEE-ZA

aircraft l'avion (m) Lah-VEE-On

airline la ligne aérienne Lah LEEN ah-A-REE-ĕN

airport l'aéroport (m) Lah-A-RO-PORB

aisle couloir KooL-Wah

all tout (m) Too   toute (f) TooT

almost presque PRĕS-Kuh

alone seul SooL

also aussi O-SEE

always toujours Too-ZHooR

ambulance l'ambulance (f) Lahñ-Bew-Lahñs

American américain (m) ah-MA-REE-Kāñ

    américaine (f) ah-MA-REE-Kĕñ

and et A

another un autre uhñ NO-TRuh

anything quelque chose KĕL-Kuh SHOZ

apartment l'appartement (m)

    Lah-Pah-Tuh-Mahñ

appetizers les hors-d'oeuvres (m/pl)

    LA ZOR-Dou-VRuh

apple la pomme Lah PuhM

appointment le rendez-vous L⓾ R⓪ñ-D④-V∞

April avril ⓪-VR㋎L

arrival l'arrivée (f) L⓪-R㋎-V④

arrive (to) arriver ⓪-R㋎-V④

ashtray le cendrier L⓾ S⓪ñ-DR㋎-④

aspirin l'aspirine (f) L⓪S-P㋎-R㋎N

attention l'attention (f) L⓪-T⓪ñ-S㋎-Öñ

August août ∞T

Australia l'Australie (f) LÖ-STR⓪-L㋎

Australian l' australien (m) LÖ-STR⓪-L㋎⓪ñ
    l'australienne (f) LÖ-STR⓪-L㋎㋎ñ

author l'auteur (m) LÖ-T⓾R

automobile l'automobile (f) LÖ-TÖ-MÖ-B㋎L

autumn l'automne LÖ-T⓾ñ

avenue l'avenue L⓪-V⓾-N⓾

awful affreux (m) ⓪-FR⓾
    affreuse (f) ⓪-FR⓾Z

B

baby le bébé L⓾ B④-B④

babysitter le garde-bébé L⓾ G⓪RD B④-B④

bacon le bacon Luh BA-Kuhn

bad mauvais (m) MO-VA mauvaise (f) MO-Vêz

bag le sac Luh Sahk

baggage les bagages (m) LA Bah-GahZH

baked au four O FooR

bakery la boulangerie Lah Boo-Lahñ-ZHuh-REE

banana la banane Lah Bah-Nahn

bandage le bandage Luh BahN-DahZH

bank la banque Lah Bahñk

barbershop le salon de coiffure

  Luh Sâ-LON Duh KWê-FewR

bartender le barman Luh BahR MahN

bath la bain Lah Bâñ

bathing suit le maillot de bains

  Luh Mah-YO Duh Bâñ

bathroom la salle de bains

  Lah Sahl Duh Bâñ

battery la batterie Luh Bah-Tuh-REE

beach la plage Lah PLahZH

beautiful beau (m) BO / belle (f) BêL

beauty shop le salon de beauté

  Luh Sâ-LOñ Duh Boo-TA

bed le lit Luh LEE

beef le boeuf Luh BOuF

beer la bière Lah BEE-eR

bellman le chasseur Luh SHah-SOuR

belt la ceinture Lah Sän-TOuR

big grand (m) GRahñ

grande (f) GRahND

bill l'addition (f) Lah-DEE-SEE-Oñ

black noir NWahR

blanket la couverture Lah KOO-VeR-TOuR

blue bleu BLou

boat le bateau Luh Bah-TO

book le livre Luh LEE-VRuh

bookstore la librairie Lah LEE-BRe-Ree

border la frontière Lah FROñ-TEE-eR

boy le garçon Luh GahR-SOñ

bracelet le bracelet Luh BRah-Suh-LA

brake le frein Luh FRahñ

bread le pain Luh Pahñ

breakfast le petit déjeuner

Luh Puh-TEE DA-ZHou-NA

broiled grillé (f) GREE-YA

brother le frère Luh FReR

brush la brosse Lah BROS

building le bâtiment Luh Bah-TEE-Mahñ

bus l'autobus (m) LO-TO-Bews

bus station la gare routière
Lah GahR Roo-TEE-eR

bus stop l'arrêt de bus (m) Lah-Re Duh Bews

business les affaires (f) LA Zah-FeR

butter le beurre Luh BouR

buy (to) acheter ahSH-Ta

C

cab le taxi Luh TahK-SEE

call (to) appeler ah-Puh-LA

camera l'appareil-photo (m)
Lah-Pah-RA FO-TO

Canada Canada Kah-Nah-Dah

Canadian Canadien (m) KahN-ah-DEEahñ
Canadienne (f) KahN-ah-DEEeñ

candy le bonbon Luh BOñ-BOñ

car la voiture Lah VWah-TewR

carrot la carotte Lah Kah-ROT

castle le château Luh SHah-TO

cathedral la cathédrale L@ K@-T@-DR@L

celebration la fête L@ F@T

center le centre L@ S@ñ-TR@

cereal les céréales L@ S@-R@-@L

chair la chaise L@ SH@Z

champagne la champagne

    L@ SH@ñ-P@N-Y@

change (to) changer SH@ñ-ZH@

change (exact) la monnaie précise

    L@ M@-N@ PR@-S@S

change (money) la monnaie L@ M@-N@

cheap bon marché B@ñ M@B-SH@

check (bill in a restaurant) l'addition (f)

    L@-D@-S@-@ñ

cheers à votre santé @-V@-TR@ S@ñ-T@

cheese le fromage L@ FR@-M@ZH

chicken le poulet L@ P@-L@

child l'enfant L@ñ-F@ñ

chocolate (flavor) au chocolat @ SH@-K@-L@

church l'église (f) L@-GL@Z

cigar le cigare L@ S@-G@B

cigarette la cigarette L@ S@-G@-R@T

city la ville L@h V€€L

clean propre PR©-PR@h

close (to) fermer F€R-M@

closed fermé F€R-M@

clothes les vêtements (m) L@ V€T-M@hñ

cocktail le cocktail L@h K@hK-T@L

coffee le café L@h K@h-F@

cold froid (m) FRW@h froide (f) FRW@hD

comb le peigne L@h P€-NY@h

come (to) venir V@h-N€€R

company (business) la compagnie

L@h K©ñ-P@h-NY€€

computer l'ordinateur L@R-D€€-N@h-T@uR

concert le concert L@h K©ñ-S€R

condom le préservatif

L@h PR@-Z€R-V@h-T€€F

conference la conférence

L@h K©ñ-F@-R@hñS

conference room la sale de conférences

L@h S@hL D@h K©ñ-F@-R@hñS

congratulations félicitations

F@-L€€-S€€-T@h-S€€-©ñ

copy machine le copieur L⒰ K⓪-P⒠-⒪R

corn le maïs L⒰ Mⓐ-⒠S

cough syrup le sirop contre la toux

　　L⒰ S⒠-R⓪ K⓪ñ-TR⒰ L⒜ T⒪

cover charge le couvert L⒰ K⒪-V⒠R

crab le crabe L⒰ KR⒜B

cream la crème L⒜ KR⒠M

credit card la carte de crédit

　　L⒜ K⒜RT D⒰ KR⒜-D⒠

cup la tasse L⒜ T⒜S

customs la douane L⒜ DW⒜N

D

dance (to) danser D⒜ñ-S⒜

dangerous dangereux (m) D⒜ñ-ZH⒰-R⒪

　　dangereuse (f) D⒜ñ-ZH⒰-R⒪S

date (calendar) la date L⒜ D⒜T

day le jour L⒰ ZH⒪R

December décembre D⒜-S⒜ñ-BR⒰

delicious délicieux (m) D⒜-L⒠-S⒠-⒪

　　délicieuse (f) D⒜-L⒠-S⒠-⒪S

delighted enchanté ⒜ñ-SH⒜ñ-T⒜

dentist le dentiste L⒰ D⒜ñ-T⒠ST

deodorant le déodorant L-D-O-DO-Rahñ

department store le grand magasin

L GRahñ Mah-Gah-Zäñ

departure le départ L DA-PahR

dessert le dessert L DA-SëR

detour le détour L DA-TooR

diabetic diabétique DEE-ah-BA-TEEK

diarrhea la diarrhée Lah DEE-ah-RA

dictionary le dictionnaire L DEEK-SEE-O-NëR

dinner le dîner L DEE-NA

dining room la salle à manger

Lah SahL ah Mahñ-ZHA

direction la direction Lah DEE-RëK-SEE-Oñ

dirty sale SahL

disabled handicapé Hahñ-DEE-Kah-PA

discount la remise Lah Ruh-MEEZ

distance la distance Lah DEES-TahñS

doctor le docteur L DahK-TooR

documents les documents (m)

LA DO-Kew-Mahñ

dollar le dollar L DO-LahR

down descendre DE-Sahñ-DRuh

downtown en ville ahñ VEEL

dress la robe LAH ROB

drink (to) boire BWAHR

drive (to) conduire KOñ-DWEER

drugstore la pharmacie LAH FAHR-MAH-SEE

dry cleaner la teinturerie LAH TAñ-Tew-E-REE

duck le canard Luh KAH-NAHR

E

ear l'oreille LO-RA-You

ear drops les gouttes pour les oreilles (f)
   LA GOOT POOR LA ZO-RA-You

early tôt TO

east l'est (m) LEST

easy facile FAH-SEEL

eat (to) manger MAHñ-ZHA

eggs l'oeuf LouF

eggs (fried) les oeufs sur le plat (m/pl)
   LA ZouF SewR Luh PLAH

eggs (scrambled) les oeufs brouillés (m/pl)
   LA ZouF BREE-YA

electricity l'électricité (f)

    LA-LEK-TREE-SEE-TA

elevator l'ascenseur (m) Lah-Sahñ-SOUR

embassy l'ambassade (f) Lahñ-Bah-SahD

emergency l'urgence (f) LOUR-ZHahñS

England l'Angleterre LahNG-Luh-TER

English anglais (m) ahñ-GLA

    anglaise (f) ahñ-GLEZ

enough! c'est assez! SA Tah-SA

entrance l'entrée (f) Lahñ-TRA

envelope l'enveloppe (f) Lahñ-Vuh-LOP

evening la soirée Lah SWah-RA

everything tout TOO

excellent excéllent (m) EK-SA-Lahñ

    excéllente (f) EK-SA-LahñT

excuse me pardon PahR-DOñ

exit la sortie Lah SOR-TEE

expensive cher SHER

eyes les yeux (m) LA ZEE-YOU

eyedrops les gouttes pour les yeux

    LA GOOT POOR LA ZEE-YOU

F

face le visage Luh VEE-SahZH

far loin LWahñ

fare (cost) le tarif Luh Tah-REEF

fast rapide Rah-PEED

fax le fax Luh FahKS

fax machine le télécopieur

    Luh TA-LA-KO-PEE-ouR

February février FA-VREE-A

few peu de Pou Duh

film (camera) la pellicule Lah PE-LEE-KewL

film (movie) le cinéma Luh SEE-NA-Mah

fine (very well) très bien TRA BEE-añ

finger le doigt Luh DWah

fire! le feu! Luh Fou

fire extinguisher l'extincteur (m)

    LEK-STañK-TouR

first premier (m) PREM-YA

    première (f) PREM-YER

fish le poisson Luh PWah-SOñ

flight le vol Luh VOL

florist shop le fleuriste Luh FLou-REEST

flowers les fleurs L& FL⊚B

food la nourriture L& N⊚-B€-T⊛B

foot le pied L⊕ PY&

fork la fourchette L& F⊚B-SH€T

France la France L& FB&ñS

French français (m) FB&ñ-S&

    française (f) FB&ñ-S€Z

French (language) le français L⊕ FB&ñ-S&

french fries les frites L& FB€T

fresh frais FB&

Friday vendredi V&ñ-DB⊕-D€

fried frit (m) FB€   frite (f) FB€T

friend l'ami (m) L&-M€   l'amie (f) L&-M€

fruit le fruit L⊕ FBW€

funny drôle DB⊚L

G

gas station la station de service

    L& ST&-S€-Oñ D⊕ S€B-V€S

gasoline l'essence (f) L€-S&ñS

gate la barrière L& B&B-€-€B

gentleman monsieur M⊕-SY⊚

gift le cadeau L⊕ K&-D⊚

girl la fille L㉐ F㋥

glass (drinking) le verre L㋿ V㋥R

glasses (eye) les lunettes L㉓ L㋎-N㋥T

gloves les gants L㉓ G㉐ñ

gold l'or L㋳R

golf le golf L㋿ G㋳LF

golf course le terrain de golf
    L㋿ T㋥-R㉐ñ D㋥ G㋳LF

good bon (m) B㋳ñ bonne (f) B㋿N

good-bye au revoir ㋳-R㋿-VW㉐R

grapes les raisins L㉓ R㉓-Z㉐ñ

grateful reconnaissant R㋿-K㋳-N㋥-S㉐ñ

gray gris (m) GR㋥ grise (f) GR㋥S

green vert (m) V㋥R verte (f) V㋥RT

grocery store l'épicerie (f) L㉓-P㋥-S㋥-R㋥

group le groupe L㋿ GR㋰P

guide le guide L㋿ G㋥D

H

hair les cheveux (m/pl) L㉓ SH㋿-V㋰

hairbrush la brosse à cheveux
    L㋿ BR㋳S ㉐ SH㋿-V㋰

haircut la coupe de cheveux

    L@ K@P D@ SH@-V@

ham le jambon L@ ZH@ñ-B@ñ

hamburger le hamburger

    L@ @M-B@R-G@R

hand la main L@ M@ñ

happy heureux (m) @-R@

    heureuse (f) @-R@S

have (I) J'ai ZH@

he il @L

head la tête L@ T@T

headache mal à la tête M@ L@ L@ T@T

health club le centre sportif

    L@ S@ñ-TR@ SP@R-T@F

heart le coeur L@ K@R

heart condition mal au coeur M@ L@-K@R

heat la chaleur L@ SH@-L@R

hello bonjour B@ñ-ZH@R

help au secours @ S@-K@R

here ici @-S@

holiday la fête L@ F@T

hospital l'hôpital (m) L@-P@-T@L

hot dog le hot dog Lⓤⓗ H◉T D◉G

hotel l'hôtel (m) L◎-T◉L

hour l'heure L◎⓾ⓡ

how comment K◎-M◎ñ

hurry! dépêchez-vous! D◉-P◉-SH◉ V◎

husband le marie (m) Lⓤⓗ M◉-ⓡ◉

I

I je ZHⓤⓗ

ice la glace L◉ GL◉S

ice cream la glace L◉ GL◉S

ice cubes le glaçons (f) L◉ GL◉-S◎ñ

ill malade M◉-L◉D

important important (m) ◉ñ-P◎ⓡ-T◉ñ
　　importante (f) ◉ñ-P◎ⓡ-T◉ñT

indigestion la dyspepsie L◉ D◉S-P◉P-S◉

information les renseignements (m/pl)
　　L◉ ⓡ◉ñ-S◉N-Yⓤⓗ-M◉ñ

inn l'auberge (f) L◎-B◉ⓡZH

interpreter l'interprète (m) L◉ñ-T◉ⓡ-Pⓡ◉T

J

jacket le veston Lⓤⓗ V◉S-T◎ñ

jam la confiture L◉ K◎ñ-F◉-Tⓔⓦⓡ

January janvier ZH@ñ-VEE-A

jewelry les bijoux (m) LA BEE-ZHoo

jewelry store la bijouterie Lah BEE-ZHoo-Tĕ-REE

job le travail Luh TRah-Vah-You

juice le jus Luh ZHoo

June juin ZHoo-@ñ

July juillet ZHoo-EE-A

K

ketchup le ketchup Luh Kĕ-CHuhP

key la clé Lah KLA

kiss le baiser Luh BA-SA

knife le couteau Luh Koo-TO

know (I) Je sais ZHuh SA

L

ladies' restroom Dames D@hM

lady la dame Lah D@hM

lamb l'agneau L@hñ-YO

language la langue Lah LahNG

large grand (m) GRahñ grande (f) GRahND

late tard TahR

laundry la blanchisserie Lᵘʰ BLᵃʰñ-SHᴇᴇ-Sᵉ̈-Bᴇᴇ

lawyer l'avocat (m) Lᵃʰ-Vⓞ-Kᵃʰ

left (direction) à gauche (f) ᵃʰ GⓄSH

leg la jambe Lᵘʰ ZHᵃʰñB

lemon le citron Lᵘʰ Sᴇᴇ-TBⓄñ

less moins MWⓐñ

letter la lettre Lᵃʰ Lᵉ̈-TBᵘʰ

lettuce la laitue Lᵃʰ LⒶ-Tᵉʷ

light la lumière Lᵃʰ LᵉʷM-Yᵉ̈B

like comme KⓄM

like (I) Je veux ZHᵘʰ Vⓞⓞ

like (I would) Je voudrais ZHᵘʰ Vⓞⓞ-DBⒶ

lip la lèvre Lᵃʰ Lᵉ̈-VBᵘʰ

lipstick le rouge Lᵘʰ BⓞⓞZH

little petit (m) Pᵘʰ-Tᴇᴇ petite (f) Pᵘʰ-TᴇᴇT

live (to) vivre Vᴇᴇ-VBᵘʰ

lobster le homard Lᵘʰ Ⓞ-MᵃʰB

long long (m) LⓄñ longue (f) LⓄNG

lost perdu Pᵉ̈B-Dᵉʷ

love l'amour Lᵃʰ-MⓞⓞB

luck la chance Lᵃʰ SHᵃʰñS

luggage les bagages (m) LA Bä-GahZH

lunch le déjeuner Luh DA-ZHou-NA

M

maid la domestique Lah DOM-ĕS-TEEK

mail le courrier Luh Koo-REE-A

makeup le maquillage Luh Mah-KEE-YahZH

man l'homme (m) LOM

manager le gérant Luh ZHA-Rahñ

map le plan Luh PLahñ

March mars MahRS

market le marché Luh MahR-SHA

match (light) l'allumette (f) Lah-Lew-MĕT

May mai MA

mayonnaise la mayonnaise Lah Mah-YO-NĕZ

meal le repas Luh Ruh-Pah

meat la viande Lah VEE-ahñD

mechanic le mécanicien
    Luh MA-Kah-NEE-SEE-äñ

medicine le médecine Luh MA-Duh-SEEN

meeting le rendez-vous Luh Rahñ-DA-Voo

mens' restroom messieurs MĕSY-SYou

menu la carte Lah KahRT

message le message L⓾ M̃ẽ-S⓪-ZH

milk le lait L⓾ Lⓐ

mineral water l'eau minérale (f)

    Lⓞ Mⓔⓔ-Nⓐ-R⓪L

minute le minute L⓾ Mⓔⓔ-N⓮T

Miss mademoiselle M⓪D-MW⓪-Z̃ẽL

mistake la faute L⓪ FⓞT

misunderstanding le malentendu

    L⓾ M⓪L-⓪ñ-T⓪ñ-D⓮

moment le moment L⓾ Mⓞ-M⓪ñ

Monday lundi L⓾ñ-Dⓔⓔ

money l'argent (m) L⓪R-ZH⓪ñ

month le mois L⓾ MW⓪

monument le monument L⓾ Mⓞ-N⓮-M⓪ñ

more plus PL⓮

morning le matin L⓾ M⓪-T⓪̃ñ

mosque la mosquée L⓪ MⓞS-Kⓐ

mother la mère L⓪ M̃ẽR

mountain la montagne L⓪ Mⓞñ-T⓪N-Y⓾

movie le cinéma L⓾ Sⓔⓔ-Nⓐ-M⓪

Mr. monsieur M⓾-SY⓸

Mrs. madame Mⓐ-DⓐM

much (too) trop TRO

museum le musée Luh Mew-ZA

mushroom le champignon
    Luh SHahñ-PEEN-YON

music la musique Lah Mew-ZEEK

mustard la moutarde Lah Moo-TahRD

N

nail polish la vernis à ongles
    Lah VeB-NEE Sah Oñ-GLuh

name le nom Luh NOñ

napkin la serviette Lah SeB-VEE-eT

near près de PRA Duh

neck le cou Luh Koo

need (I) J'ai besoin ZHA Buh-ZWañ

never jamais ZHah-MA

newspaper le journal Luh ZHooB-NahL

news stand le kiosque Luh KEE-ahSK

night la nuit Lah NWEE

nightclub la boite de nuit
    Lah BWahT Duh NWEE

no non NOñ

no smoking non fumeurs NOñ Few-MooB

noon midi MEE-DEE

north le nord Luh NOR

notary le notaire Luh NO-TeR

November novembre NO-Vahñ-BRuh

now maintenant Mañ-Tuh-Nahñ

number le numéro Luh New-MA-RO

nurse l'infirmière (f) Lañ-FeR-MEE-eR

O

occupied occupé O-Kew-PA

ocean l'océan (m) LO-SA-ahñ

October octobre OK-TO-BRuh

officer l'officier (m) LO-FEE-SEE-A

oil l'huile (f) Lew-EEL

omelet l'omelette (f) LOM-LeT

one way (traffic) sens unique SahñS ew-NEEK

onions les oignons LA ZO-NYOñ

open (to) ouvrir oo-VReeR

opera l'opéra (m) LO-PA-Rah

operator le standardiste Luh STahN-Dahr-DEEST

optician l'opticien LOP-TEE-SEE-ahñ

orange (color) orange Ⓞ-Ⓡⓐⓝ-ZH

orange (fruit) l'orange (f) LⓄ-ⓇⓐⓝZH

order (to) commander KⓄ-Mⓐⓝ-DⒶ

original original Ⓞ-ⓇⒺ-ZHⒺⒺ-NⓐL

owner le propriétaire LⓊ PⓇⓄ-PⓇⒺ-Yⓔ-TⓔⓇ

oysters les huîtres (f/pl) LⒶ ẒWⒺⒺ-TⓇⓊ

P

package le paquet LⓊ Pⓐ-Kⓔ

paid payé PⒶ-YⒶ

pain la douleur Lⓐ DⓄⓄ-LⓄⓤⓇ

painting la peinture Lⓐ Pⓐⓝ-TⓔⓦⓇ

pantyhose le collant LⓊ KⓄ-Lⓐⓝ

paper le papier LⓊ Pⓐ-PⒺⒺ-Ⓐ

park (to) stationner STⓐ-SⒺⒺ-Ⓞ-NⒶ

park le parc LⓊ PⓐⓇK

partner (business) associé ⓐ-SⓄ-SⒺⒺ-Ⓐ

party la soirée Lⓐ SWⓐ-ⓇⒶ

passenger le passager LⓊ Pⓐ-Sⓐ-ZHⒶ

passport le passeport LⓊ PⓐS-PⓄⓇ

pasta les pâtes LⒶ PⓐT

pastries les pâtisseries　L�� P⓪-T⒠-S⒠-R⒠

pen le stylo　L⓾ ST⒠-L⓪

pencil le crayon　L⓾ KRⓐ-Y⓪ñ

pepper le poivre　L⓾ PW⓪-VR⓾

perfume le parfum　L⓾ P⓪R-F⓾ñ

person la personne　L⓪ P⒠R-S⓪N

pharmacist le pharmacien

    L⓾ F⓪R-M⓪-S⒠-⓪ñ

pharmacy la pharmacie　L⓪ F⓪R-M⓪-S⒠

phone book l'annuaire　L⓪-N⒠ⱳ-⒠R

photo la photo　Lⓐ F⓪-T⓪

photographer le photographier

    L⓾ F⓪-T⓪-GR⓪-F⒠-ⓐ

pie la tarte　L⓪ T⓪RT

pillow l'oreiller (m)　L⓪-Rⓐ-Yⓐ

pink rose　R⓪Z

pizza la pizza　L⓪ P⒠D-S⓪

plastic le plastique　L⓾ PL⓪S-T⒠K

plate l'assiette (f)　L⓪-S⒠-⒠T

please s'il vous plaît　S⒠L V⓪⓪ PL⒠

pleasure le plaisir Luh PLé-ZeR

police la police Lah PO-LeeS

police station la poste de police

    Lah POST Duh Puh-LeeS

pork le porc Luh POR

porter le porteur Luh POR-TouR

post office la poste Lah POST

postcard la carte postale Lah KahBT POS-TahL

potato la pomme de terre Lah PuhM Duh TéB

pregnant enceinte ahñ-SäñT

prescription la prescription

    Lah PBé-SKBeeP-See-Oñ

price le prix Luh PBee

problem le problème Luh PBO-BLéM

profession la profession Lah PBO-Fé-See-ON

public publique PewB-LeeK

public telephone le téléphone publique

    Luh TA-LA-FON PewB-LeeK

purified purifié PewB-ee-Fee-A

purple violet (m) Vee-O-LA

    violette (f) Vee-O-LéT

purse le sac Luh SahK

Q

quality la qualité L@h K@h-L@-T@

question la question L@h K@S-T@-O@ñ

quickly rapidement R@h-P@D-M@ñ

quiet (be) taisez-vous T@-Z@ V@

quiet tranquille TR@ñ-K@L

R

radio la radio L@h R@hD-Y@

railroad le chemin de fer L@ SH@-M@ñ D@ F@R

rain la pluie L@h PL@-@

raincoat l'imperméable (m)

   L@ñ-P@R-M@-@B-L@

ramp la rampe L@h R@hMP

rare (cooked) saignant S@-NY@ñ

razor blades les lames de rasoir

   L@ L@hM D@ R@h-SW@hR

ready prêt PR@

receipt le reçu L@ R@h-S@

recommend (to) recommander

   R@h-K@-M@ñ-D@

red rouge R@ZH

repeat répéter R@-P@-T@

reservation la réservation

    Lah RA-ZeR-Vah-SEE-Oñ

restaurant le restaurant   Luh ReS-TO-Rahñ

return revenir   Ruh-Vuh-NEER

return (to give back) revenir   Ruh-Vuh-NEER

rice le riz   Luh REE

rich riche   REESH

right (correct) correct   KO-ReKT

right (direction) à droite   ah DRWahT

road le chemin   Luh SHuh-Mañ

room la chambre   Lah SHahñ-BRuh

round trip l'aller et retour   Lah-LA A Ruh-TooR

S

safe (hotel) le coffre-fort   Luh KO-FRuh FOR

salad la salade   Lah Sah-LahD

sale la vente   Lah VahñT

salmon le saumon   Luh Suh-MOñ

salt le sel   Luh SeL

sandwich le sandwich   Luh Sahñ-WEECH

Saturday samedi   Sah-Muh-DEE

scissors les ciseaux (m)   LA SEE-ZO

sculpture la sculpture   Lah SKewLP-TewR

seafood les fruits de mer (m)

  L@ FRW@@ D@h M@R

season la saison L@h S@-Z@ñ

seat la place L@h PL@hS

secretary la secrétaire L@h S@-KR@-T@R

section la section L@h S@K-S@@-@@ñ

September septembre S@P-T@hñ-BR@h

service le service L@h S@R-V@@S

several plusieurs PL@w-ZY@R

shampoo le shampooing L@h SH@hñ-P@@-@N

sheets (bed) les draps L@ DR@h

shirt la chemise L@h SH@h-M@@S

shoe la chaussure L@h SH@-S@wR

shoe store la boutique de chaussures

   L@h B@@-T@@K D@h SH@-S@wR

shop la boutique L@h B@@-T@@K

shopping center le centre commercial

   L@h S@hñ-TR@h K@-M@R-S@@-@hL

shower la douche L@h D@@SH

shrimp les crevettes L@ KR@h-V@T

sick malade M@h-L@hD

sign (display) le signe L@h S@@N-Y@h

signature la signature L@h S@EN-Y@h-T@wB

single seul S@uL

sir monsieur M@h-SY@u

sister la soeur L@h S@uB

size la taille L@h T@A-Y@u

skin la peau L@A P@O

skirt la jupe L@h ZH@ooP

sleeve la manche L@h M@hñSH

slowly lentement L@hñ-T@h-M@hñ

small petit (m) P@h-T@EE
    petite (f) P@h-T@EET

smile (to) sourire S@oo-B@EEB

smoke (to) fumer F@ew-M@A

soap le savon L@h S@h-V@Oñ

socks les chaussettes L@A SH@O-S@ëT

some quelque K@ëL-K@h

something quelque chose K@ëL-K@h SH@OZ

sometimes quelquefois K@ëL-K@h-FW@h

soon bientôt B@EE-@añ-T@O

sorry (I am) Je suis désolé
    ZH@h SW@EE D@A-S@O-L@A

soup la soupe L@h S@ooP

south le sud L⑩ S⑳D

souvenir le souvenir L⑩ S⑳-V⑩-N⑤R

speciality la spécialité L⑧ SP④-S⑤-⑧-L⑤-T④

spoon la cuillère L⑧ KW⑤-⑥R

spring (season) le printemps L⑩ PR⑧ñ-T⑧ñ

stairs les escaliers L④ Z⑥-SK⑧L-Y④

stamp le timbre L⑩ T⑧ñ-BR⑩

station la gare L⑧ G⑧R

steak le bifteck L⑩ B⑤F-T⑥K

steamed à l'etuvée ⑧ L④-T⑳-V④

stop arrêtez ⑧-R⑥-T④

store le magasin L⑩ M⑧-G⑧-Z⑧ñ

straight ahead tout droit T⑳ DRW⑧

strawberry la fraise L⑧ FR⑥Z

street la rue L⑧ R⑳

string la ficelle L⑧ F⑤-S⑥L

subway le métro L⑩ M④-TR⑩

sugar le sucre L⑩ S⑳-KR⑩

suit (clothes) le complet L⑩ K⑩ñ-PL⑥

suitcase la valise L⑧ V⑧-L⑤S

summer l'été L④-T④

sun le soleil Luh SO-LA

Sunday dimanche DEE-MahñSH

sunglasses les lunettes de soleil (f/pl)

    LA Lew-NēT Duh SO-LA

suntan lotion la lotion à bronzer

    Lah LO-SEE-Oñ ah BROñ-ZA

supermarket le supermarché

    Luh Sew-PēR-MahR-SHA

surprise la surprise Lah SewR-PREEZ

sweet doux Doo

swim (to) nager Nah-ZHA

swimming pool la piscine Lah PEE-SEEN

synagogue la synagogue Lah SEE-Nah-GOG

T

table la table Lah Tah-BLuh

tampons les tampons LA Tahñ-POñ

tape (sticky) le ruban Luh Rew-Bahñ

tape recorder le magnétophone

    Luh Mah-NA-TO-FON

tax la taxe Lah TahKS

taxi le taxi Lⓤⱨ TⓐK-Sⓔⓔ

tea le thé Lⓤⱨ Tⓐ

telegram le télégramme Lⓤⱨ Tⓐ-Lⓐ-GRⓐⱨM

telephone le téléphone Lⓤⱨ Tⓐ-Lⓐ-FⓄN

television la télévision Lⓐⱨ Tⓐ-Lⓐ-Vⓔⓔ-Sⓔⓔ-Ⓞñ

temperature la température

　　Lⓐⱨ Tⓐⱨñ-Pⓔ-Rⓐⱨ-TⓔⱳR

temple le temple Lⓤⱨ Tⓐⱨñ-PLⓤⱨ

tennis la tennis Lⓐⱨ Tⓔ-NⓔⓔS

tennis court le terrain de tennis

　　Lⓤⱨ Tⓔ-Rⓐñ Dⓤⱨ Tⓔ-NⓔⓔS

thank you merci MⓔR-Sⓔⓔ

that cela Sⓤⱨ-Lⓐⱨ

the le (m) Lⓤⱨ

　　la (f) Lⓐⱨ

theater le théâtre Lⓤⱨ Tⓐ-ⱨ-TRⓤⱨ

there là Lⓐⱨ

they ils ⓔⓔL

this ce / cet / cette Sⓤⱨ / SⓔT / SⓔT

thread le fil Lⓤⱨ FⓔⓔL

throat la gorge Lⓐⱨ GⓄRZH

Thursday jeudi ZHⓞⱶ-Dⓔⓔ

ticket le billet Luh BEE-YA

tie la cravate Lah KRah-VahT

time l'heure LouR

tip (gratuity) le pourboire Luh PooR-BWahR

tire (car) le pneu Luh Puh-Nou

tired fatigué Fah-TEE-GA

toast pain grillé Pañ GREE-YA

tobacco le tabac Luh Tah-Bah

today aujourd'hui O-ZHooR-DWEE

toe l'orteil LOR-TA

together ensemble añ-Sañ-BLuh

toilet la toilette Lah TWah-LëT

toilet paper le papier hygiénique

Luh Pah-PEE-A EE-ZHEE-A-NEEK

tomato la tomate Lah TO-MahT

tomorrow demain Duh-Mañ

toothache le mal aux dents Luh MahL O Dañ

toothbrush la brosse à dents

Lah BROS ah Dañ

toothpaste le dentifrice Luh Dañ-TEE-FREES

toothpick le cure-dents Luh KewR Dañ

tour la visite Lah VEE-ZEET

tourist　le touriste　L⓪ T⓪-RⓔST

tourist office　le bureau de tourisme

　　L⓪ Bⓔw-R⓪ D⓪ T⓪-RⓔS-M⓪

towel　la serviette　Lⓐ SⓔR-Vⓔ-ⓔT

train　le train　L⓪ TRⓐñ

travel agency　l'agence de voyage

　　Lⓐ-ZHⓐñS D⓪ VWⓐ-Yⓐ ZH

traveler's check　le chèque de voyage

　　L⓪ SHⓔK D⓪ VWⓐ-Yⓐ ZH

trip　le voyage　L⓪ VWⓐ-Yⓐ ZH

trousers　le pantalon　L⓪ Pⓐñ-Tⓐ-Lⓞñ

trout　la truite　Lⓐ TRWⓔw-ⓔT

truth　la vérité　Lⓐ Vⓐ-Rⓔ-Tⓐ

Tuesday　mardi　MⓐR-Dⓔ

turkey　la dinde　Lⓐ DⓐñND

U

umbrella　la parapluie　Lⓐ Pⓐ-Rⓐ-PLⓔw-ⓔ

understand (to)　comprendre　KⓞN-PRⓐñ-DR⓪

underwear　les sous-vêtements

　　Lⓐ Sⓞ VⓔT-Mⓐñ

United Kingdom　Royaume-Uni

　　Rⓞy-ⓞM ⓞ-Nⓔ

United States les Etats-Unis

   L(A) Z(A)-T(ah)-Z(ew)-N(EE)

university l'université (f) L(ew)-N(EE)-V(ê)R-S(EE)-T(A)

up haut (O)

urgent urgent (ew)R-ZH(ah)ñ

V

vacancies (accommodation) chambres libres (f/pl)

   SH(ah)ñ-BR(uh) L(EE)-BR(uh)

vacation les vacances L(A) V(ah)-K(ah)ñS

valuable précieux (m) PR(A)-SY(ou)

   précieuse (f) PR(A)-SY(ou)S

value le valeur L(uh) V(ah)-L(ou)R

vanilla la vanille L(ah) V(ah)-N(EE)

veal le veau L(uh) V(O)

vegetables les légumes (m) L(A) L(A)-G(ew)M

view la vue L(ah) V(ew)

vinegar le vinaigre L(uh) V(EE)-N(A)-GR(uh)

voyage le voyage L(uh) VW(ah)-Y(ah)ZH

W

wait attendez (ah)-T(ah)ñ-D(A)

waiter le garçon L(uh) G(ah)R-S(O)ñ

waitress la serveuse L(ah) S(ê)R-V(ou)S

want (I) Je voudrais ZH⑩ V⑩-DR④

wash (to) laver L⑨-V④

watch (time piece) la montre L⑨ M⑥ñ-TR⑩

watch out! attention ⑨-T⑨ñ-S㊉-⑥ñ

water l'eau L⑩

we nous N⑩

weather le temps L⑩ T⑨ñ

Wednesday mercredi M㊉R-KR⑩-D㊉

week la semaine L⑨ S⑩-M㊉N

weekend le week-end L⑩ W㊉K-⑥ND

welcome bienvenu B㊉-④ñ-V㊉-N⑩

well done (cooked) bien cuit B㊉-⑨ñ KW㊉

west l'ouest L⑩-⑥ST

what? que? / quoi? K⑩ / KW⑨

wheelchair le fauteuil roulant

L⑩ F⑥-T⑩-Y⑩ R⑩-L⑨ñ

when? quand? K⑨ñ

where? où? ⑩

which? quel? / quelle K㊉L

white blanc (m) BL⑨ñ / blanche (f) BL⑨ñSH

who? qui? K㊉

why? pourquoi? P∞R-KW@

wife la femme L@ F@M

wind le vent L@ V@ñ

window la fenêtre L@ F@-N@-TR@

wine le vin L@ V@ñ

wine list la carte de vins L@ K@RT D@ V@ñ

winter l'hiver L@-V@R

with avec @-V@K

woman la femme L@ F@M

wonderful merveilleux M@R-V@-Y@

world le monde L@ M@ñD

wrong avoir tort @-VW@R T@R

XYZ

year l'année L@-N@

yellow jaune ZH@N

yes oui W@

yesterday hier Y@R

you tu / vous T@ / V∞

zipper la fermeture L@ F@R-M@-T@R

zoo le zoo L@ Z@

EASILY PRONOUNCED
LANGUAGE SYSTEMS

Author Clyde Peters graduated from Radford High School and the University of Hawaii and has traveled the world as a travel writer. His innovative Say It Right phrase books have revolutionized the way languages are taught and learned. Mr. Peters invented the Vowel Symbol System for easy and correct pronunciation of virtually any language. He currently continues traveling the world working on new languages and divides his spare time between Las Vegas, Nevada, and Hawaii.

Betty Chapman is a successful business woman who along with Mr. Peters founded Easily Pronounced Language Systems to promote education, travel, and custom tailored language solutions. "Moving beyond expectation to acquisition and accomplishment is possible with EPLS."

Priscilla Leal Bailey is the senior series editor for all Say It Right products and has proved indispensable in editing and implementing the EPLS Vowel Symbol System. We are forever grateful for her belief and support.

SAY IT RIGHT SERIES
Infinite Destinations
One Pronunciation System!

Audio Editions

Say It Right App on iTunes

THANKS!

The nicest thing you can say to anyone in any language is "Thank you." Try some of these languages using the incredible EPLS Vowel Symbol System.

Arabic
SH(oo)-KR(ah)N

Chinese
SH(EE)(ě) SH(EE)(ě)

French
M(ě)R-S(EE)

German
D(ah)N-K(uh)

Hawaiian
M(ah)-H(ah)́-L(O)

Italian
GR(ah)́T-S(EE)-(ě)

Japanese
D(O)-M(O)

Portuguese
(O)-BR(EE)-G(ah)́-D(O)

Russian
SP(ah)-S(EE)-B(ah)

Spanish
GR(ah)́-S(EE)-(ah)S

Swahili
(ah)-S(ah)́N-T(A)

Tagalog
S(ah)-L(ah)-M(ah)́T

180

INDEX

QUICK REFERENCE PAGE

Hello

Bonjour

BOñ ZHOOB

Good-bye

Au revoir

O Ruh-VWahB

How are you?

Comment allez-vous?

KO-MOñ Tah-LA-VOO

Fine / Very well

Très bien

TRA BEE-äN

Yes

Oui

WEE

No

Non

NOñ

Please

S'il vous plaît

SEEL VOO PLé

Thank you

Merci

MéR-SEE

I would like...

Je voudrais...

ZHuh VOO-DRA...

Where is...

Où est...

OO A...

I don't understand!

Je ne comprends pas!

ZHOON-uh KOñ-PRahñ Pah

Help!

Au secours!

O Suh-KOOB